Cambridge Elements

Elements in Creativity and Imagination
edited by
Anna Abraham
University of Georgia, USA

THE IMAGINATION PULSE

*From Flickers to Firestorms
in Reading*

Sarah Bro Trasmundi
University of Southern Denmark

Shaftesbury Road, Cambridge CB2 8EA, United Kingdom

One Liberty Plaza, 20th Floor, New York, NY 10006, USA

477 Williamstown Road, Port Melbourne, VIC 3207, Australia

314–321, 3rd Floor, Plot 3, Splendor Forum, Jasola District Centre, New Delhi – 110025, India

103 Penang Road, #05–06/07, Visioncrest Commercial, Singapore 238467

Cambridge University Press is part of Cambridge University Press & Assessment, a department of the University of Cambridge.

We share the University's mission to contribute to society through the pursuit of education, learning and research at the highest international levels of excellence.

www.cambridge.org
Information on this title: www.cambridge.org/9781009528436
DOI: 10.1017/9781009528450

© Sarah Bro Trasmundi 2025

This publication is in copyright. Subject to statutory exception and to the provisions of relevant collective licensing agreements, no reproduction of any part may take place without the written permission of Cambridge University Press & Assessment.

When citing this work, please include a reference to the DOI 10.1017/9781009528450

First published 2025

A catalogue record for this publication is available from the British Library

ISBN 978-1-009-52843-6 Hardback
ISBN 978-1-009-52846-7 Paperback
ISSN 2752-3950 (online)
ISSN 2752-3942 (print)

Cambridge University Press & Assessment has no responsibility for the persistence or accuracy of URLs for external or third-party internet websites referred to in this publication and does not guarantee that any content on such websites is, or will remain, accurate or appropriate.

For EU product safety concerns, contact us at Calle de José Abascal, 56, 1°, 28003 Madrid, Spain, or email eugpsr@cambridge.org

The Imagination Pulse

From Flickers to Firestorms in Reading

Elements in Creativity and Imagination

DOI: 10.1017/9781009528450
First published online: July 2025

Sarah Bro Trasmundi
University of Southern Denmark
Author for correspondence: Sarah Bro Trasmundi, sarbro@sdu.dk

Abstract: This Element explores the transformative power of reading as a deeply imaginative, embodied process. It challenges conventional views of reading as mere decoding and argues that reading involves a dynamic interplay between perception, imagination, and the body. Drawing from ecological-embodied theories and cross-disciplinary insights, it introduces the concept of 'breaks' in reading – moments of pause, disruption, and reflection – as essential to fostering rich imaginative engagement. By focusing on multiscalar attention, pacemaking, and material engagement, the Element proposes a novel framework for understanding reading as an active, creative process that enhances cognitive and emotional depth. Through a cognitive ethnography of reading, the Element demonstrates how these imaginative breaks can cultivate more meaningful and sustained interactions with texts, offering insights for education and reading practices. Ultimately, the Element seeks to reimagine the role of reading in enhancing imaginative capacities and navigating today's complex social and global challenges.

This Element also has a video abstract: www.cambridge.org/ECAI-BroTrasmundi

Keywords: embodied imagination, reading, breaks, embodied cognition, cognitive ethnography

© Sarah Bro Trasmundi 2025

ISBNs: 9781009528436 (HB), 9781009528467 (PB), 9781009528450 (OC)
ISSNs: 2752-3950 (online), 2752-3942 (print)

Contents

Introduction: The Imaginative Power of Reading   1

1 Why Imagining? Why Reading?   8

2 Breaks and Their Role in Imaginative Reading   23

3 A Cognitive Ethnography of Breaks in Imaginative Reading   34

4 Reading the Future   59

References   67

Introduction: The Imaginative Power of Reading

> Reading, then, is not an automatic process of capturing a text in the way photosensitive paper captures light, but a bewildering, labyrinthine, common and yet personal process of reconstruction. Whether reading is independent from, for instance, listening, whether it is a single distinctive set of psychological processes or consists of a great variety of such processes, researchers don't yet know, but many believe that its complexity may be as great as that of thinking itself … To completely analyze what we do when we read … would almost be the acme of the psychologist's achievements, for it would be to describe very many of the most intricate workings of the human mind. We are still far from an answer.
>
> - Manguel, 2014:39

This Element emerges from both concern and hope for a more imaginative future. Today, our collective global mindset is under immense strain – challenged by the relentless pace of modern life and the pressures of constant adaptation. Our capacity for imagination seems to be diminishing, stifled by the constant demands for growth, productivity, and the pursuit of ever-smarter solutions (Collini, 2018). Yet, I remain hopeful that we can develop a slower, more deliberate mode of agency – one that strengthens attentional sensitivity and incorporates the concept of breaks. By embracing breaks, such as pauses and shifts in attention, we can learn to attend to details and processes that are often overlooked in our drive for optimisation and task completion.

The Element does not aim to offer prescriptive solutions or ready-made guidelines to the global problems and crises we experience. Instead, it invites readers to focus on the processes of imagining, and by doing so, we can become better equipped to engage intelligently and creatively with both our own agency and the complex local and global challenges we face.

While many activities, such as walking in nature or listening to music, can enhance what I call 'attentional sensitivity', reading, I argue, offers a particularly unique opportunity to refine this capacity. It refers to our ability to perceive and respond to subtle changes and details in our surroundings – whether physical, emotional, or intellectual. It involves a heightened awareness of sensorimotor experiences, such as how we hear, see, or feel the world around us. Activities like nature walks and music are powerful because they naturally engage multiple senses. Walking in nature, for example, can heighten our awareness of the shifting sounds of birds, the texture of leaves, and the rhythm of our footsteps, embedding our whole beings in the environment (Ingold, 2022). Similarly, music engages us by drawing our attention to intricate sound patterns, harmonies, and emotional undertones, fostering a heightened state of rhythmic awareness (Høffding, 2018). In both reading and nature walking, we can pause, reflect, and control the pace of our engagement, whether it is stopping to observe a tree or lingering on a passage in a book. This pacemaking mechanism makes reading closely related to nature walking, where we, as participants, set the rhythm of our experience. While textual style influences pacing, readers still play a central role in shaping their own rhythm of engagement (Popova & Cuffari, 2018). In contrast, listening to music offers a different quality of engagement – one of absorption – where we surrender control over the unfolding of sound, allowing the music to guide us. Music's continuous progression can absorb us, to the extent where we relinquish control of the pacemaking (Høffding, 2018). However, both reading and walking in nature offer a unique combination of agency and absorption. But unlike a nature walk, where one can physically move to explore a tree from multiple angles, modern alphabetic reading unfolds within a framework of picture-like, linguistic symbols (cf. Cowley, 2011). A reader cannot explore the written symbol the same way they would explore natural objects in nature. Because the information of the written marks is fixed and finite, the perceiver is unable to literally move around them and observe new details. A text is somehow like a picture, which is, 'a surface, so treated that it makes available a limited optic array of some sort at a point of observation' (Gibson, 1979:270). Interestingly, pictures, and I argue written texts, open up the possibility for a complex form of perception, that is, a double perception that merges perception and imagination. Gibson further reasons that 'a picture always requires two kinds of apprehension that go on at the same time, one direct and the other indirect. There is direct perceiving of the picture surface along with indirect awareness of virtual surface–a perceiving knowing, or imagining' (Gibson, 1979:283). While letters do not depict or represent real surfaces in the same way as a picture, they form a symbolic surface, enabling a dual mode of perception: a direct perception of their physical shapes and an indirect perception (perceiving knowing or imagining) of their symbolic basis and value; a claim that will be explored in depth in Section 1. Further, readers are free to project their lived experiences onto the symbolic framework of texts, weaving together written marks and symbolic-creative thought. This balance of structure and imaginative freedom in reading provides a powerful space for sustained cognitive and emotional engagement. While both nature walking and reading cultivate perceptual awareness, reading offers the additional benefit of training sustained focus and attention control to the activity of reading. Unlike the open-ended experience of moving through a natural landscape, reading requires continuous engagement with symbolic structures, encouraging cognitive endurance and concentration.

Pacemaking and breaks play a crucial role in preventing reading from becoming a mere act of rule-following. By consciously modulating our reading pace, we can engage with complex ideas, emotions, and scenarios, allowing for extended imaginative processes to unfold. In this way, reading not only fuels our imaginative capacity, enabling us to read beyond the lines, but also strengthens our ability to concentrate, ultimately enriching both our interaction with literature and our broader experience of life and its possibilities.

But why do I believe so strongly that reading can change us and spark the imagination in exceptional ways? Think of yourself as a reader. As you read, your entire being is engaged in a remarkable process. Modern alphabetic reading draws on lived experiences, normative attentional practices, literary techniques, and material engagement that shape not only ideas but entire ways of understanding one's world (Manguel, 2014). But this understanding is not a given. Reading research often suggests that reading is a mechanical process, explained by mapping symbolic recognition and neural pathways. But what if reading is far more than just absorbing and translating textual information? Fortunately, several colleagues are currently exploring that path (i.e. Popova & Cuffari, 2018; Di Paolo et al., 2018; Kukkonen, 2020; Mangen, 2008; Ingold, 2024; Cowley, 2021), and my perspective both builds upon and expands their work. Further, it is important to acknowledge that there are frameworks, such as Transportation Theory (Gerrig, 1993; Green & Brock, 2000, 2002), which explore the immersive and transformative dimensions of the reading. These models highlight how narrative engagement allows readers to be psychologically transported into a story world, shaping their comprehension and emotional involvement. However, even within these perspectives, reading is often framed primarily as a cognitive or affective state induced by narrative structure. Building on and extending such perspectives, this Element argues that reading is not solely about narratives, nor is it a disembodied cognitive process occurring 'in the head'. Instead, it is an interactive, multimodal practice that unfolds through affective resonance and embodied engagement with material-symbolic text. My critique does not suggest that current models entirely ignore bodily dimensions; rather, they have often treated them as secondary to cognitive processing and symbolic representation. In contrast, 4E cognition (Menary, 2010; Newen et al., 2018) challenges this view, emphasising that cognition is not confined to the brain but is shaped by the whole body's interaction with a socio-material context. This 4E framework – viewing cognition as embodied, embedded, enactive, and extended – provides a lens through which to understand the role of breaks and embodied engagement in reading. It allows for reading to be an imaginative, transformative experience – one that changes you not just intellectually but as a person. That is, it can alter how you engage with and understand the world by enhancing your attentional sensitivity to previously unnoticed details, shaping new habitual ways of experiencing the world: Reading is an education in attentional sensitivity, which impacts our imagining.

Breaks, as I will further elaborate in Section 2, are ruptures and changes in the flow of engagement that disrupt anticipatory dynamics, creating opportunities for new patterns to emerge. Here, I focus specifically on self-elicited breaks during reading – those initiated by the reader as part of the engagement process – rather than external disturbances such as email notifications or other involuntary interruptions beyond the reader's control. Empirically, breaks manifest as pauses, gaps, shifts in bodily rhythms, or changes in modes of engagement, allowing the reader to reorient and explore alternative possibilities. These breaks – whether they are pauses in the narrative, slower forms of attending, or moments of reflection — further represent a sweet spot where the boundaries between the immaterial and the observable dissolve. This oscillation between immersion and pause mirrors the principles of navigation, where skilled practitioners rely on continuously emergent perceptual information to recalibrate movement and orientation (Heft, 1996; Hutchins, 1995). Just as wayfinding involves detecting environmental structures to adjust the trajectory in real time rather than following a fixed internal map, reading involves attentional shifts that dynamically guide engagement and understanding. In both cases, action and perception are intertwined, which means that activities such as navigation and reading unfold through continuous recalibration, shaped by what the situation affords the individual. Rather than dividing the inner world of imagination from the outer world of action, breaks create a space of access where the *process* of imagining becomes experientially rich and perceptible. These moments reveal that imagination is not confined to an internal, abstract realm but is actively enacted within the flow of engagement. Especially – but not exclusively – breaks during reading provide a temporal opening where the imaginative process can be sensed, reflected upon, and even modulated, making its dynamics momentarily available to awareness. That is, in reading, self-elicited breaks are not empty pauses. They are moments where cognitive and emotional work emerges, often overlooked as non-reading moments (when a reader stops) or places of decreasing attention (when the reading pace is significantly slowed down or porous). But in these breaks, we are not stepping out of reading; rather, we are magnifying its imaginative power. These dynamic moments allow imagining to percolate, becoming possible and observable through actions like turning a page, breathing heavily, shifting position, gazing up, or changing attention and rhythm. Thus, self-elicited breaks in reading are not task interruptions; they are integral moments where engagement, understanding, and transformation unfold.

This Element presents a descriptive account, grounded in empirical observations, of how readers interact with texts, revealing the role of breaks and shifting rhythms – patterns rarely examined systematically in natural settings. Exploratory and playful reading behaviours, particularly powerful in early childhood, illustrate how readers momentarily depart from strict linearity and use breaks to strengthen understanding. While breaks are always present in reading, a reader can learn to magnify or minimise them. When minimised, the reader maintains a predictable reading pattern; one that slavishly follows the imposed flow of a text's structure, design, and narrative. This form of reading often stems from cultural and pedagogical approaches that prioritise fluency and efficiency at the expense of unpredictable, messy, and time-expensive strategies. Over time, open-ended and creative reading strategies are frequently discouraged in favour of uninterrupted, fluent textual comprehension. This development is not neutral; it shapes how reading is experienced and how imagination is either nurtured or constrained through guided behaviour and attention. Importantly, not all reading is equally rich in its imaginative potential. Dewey argues in relation to education that: 'the belief that all genuine education comes about through experience, does not mean that all experiences are genuinely or equally educative. Experience and education cannot be directly equated to each other. For some experiences are mis-educative. . . . Everything depends on the quality of the experience which is had' (Dewey, 1997:25, 27). In this case, it means that not all imaginative reading is equally rich. Therefore, there is a need to understand better, how rich imagining emerges and thrives both in relation to experience and understanding.

Again, while 4E approaches to reading are emerging, the correlation between breaks and the imaginative power of reading remains underexplored, particularly in relation to the function of breaks *during* the reading process itself. While there are multiple ways of reading, this particular style, where breaks and ruptures contribute to imaginative engagement, has been largely overlooked. Research on pauses in reading does exist, but it is largely framed within cognitive and psycholinguistic models that primarily examine pauses as indicators of processing difficulty, cognitive load, or fluency breakdowns (Wolters et al., 2022; Zermiani et al., 2024). These approaches overlook the role of pauses as an integral, strategic part of reading in relation to imagination, affect, and embodied interaction with the text. In this sense, while pauses have been studied extensively in relation to cognitive functions, such as working memory and reading comprehension, their role in shaping the reader's bodily experience, attentional sensitivity, and creative engagement deserves much closer attention.

Building on this enigma – the imaginative power of reading – this Element explores three interconnected themes: imagination, reading, and breaks. Its central argument is that the imaginative power of reading thrives through self-elicited breaks. A break-probing epistemology expands upon traditional cognitive models by offering a broader conception of reading. This alternative approach promotes an attitude that encourages a dynamic reading pace, thoughtful pauses, and rich bodily engagement with the text. The metaphor for this understanding is 'the imagination pulse', emphasising the dynamic and rhythmic nature of bodily engaging with a text. Such dynamic engagement goes beyond a linguistic translation level and fosters a creative understanding as the reader imagines with and through the text in ways that require temporal modulation of the overall activity.

Overall, this Element argues for an empirical and theoretical exploration of reading to systematically understand and nurture its imaginative power. By uncovering how readers can magnify and harness breaks for imaginative potential, we can rethink normative teaching approaches and cultivate broader skills in imaginative thinking and agency. To grasp this potential, it draws on social anthropology to examine how mainstream reading models globally (i) generate narrow conceptions of both imagining and reading, (ii) negatively impact how reading is taught, assessed, and perceived in education, and (iii) inhibit dynamic and bold imaginative processes in reading. Additionally, it employs cognitive ethnography to describe how multiple timescales intertwine in reading, demonstrating how both normative guidance and sensorimotor actions shape ontogenetic, developmental as well as experiential processes. This interplay contributes to making individuals social readers with distinct personal styles. It is further explored why readers within similar cultural and contextual settings struggle in different ways to engage in a rich imaginative reading mode, experiencing reading as anything from rigid rule-following to a transformative act. It examines both dysfunctional and functional reading modes, identifying effective bodily strategies for achieving a heightened and rich imaginative reading experience.

The Element is structured around four sections: **Section 1** establishes the importance of both imagination and reading. It argues that rich imaginative reading depends on a specific form of attention related to slower forms of engagement, which is apparently at odds with most forms of modern life.

Section 2 presents a theory of imaginative reading that integrates the importance of breaks. It suggests that rich imaginative reading is particularly salient around breaks or changes in reading. The section draws on the Japanese dramaturgy of temporal modulation to justify that temporal shifts are important for imagination. This dramaturgy has evolved into a philosophy of temporality that emphasises 'ma', a Japanese word for moments in-between, or pure duration, including processes like waiting, hesitation, and mind-wandering. Using this break-epistemology and temporal philosophy, the section outlines three defining properties of imaginative reading theory: (i) multiscalar attention, (ii) pacemaking, and (iii) material engagement.

Section 3 introduces cognitive ethnography as a framework to empirically study imaginative reading in non-experimental settings. It presents case studies and observational data of how readers navigate and benefit from dynamic, responsive reading trajectories, or (fails to) exploit the potential of pacemaking, ultimately enriching our understanding of the imaginative power of reading. The section does *not* intend to showcase what reading is like in most cases, instead, it selects cases that illustrate the idea of breaks for imaginative reading, as this aspect of reading has not been systematically explored.

Section 4 outlines the next steps for reading research and practical applications of the insights gained, particularly in educational contexts. It argues that a greater understanding of imaginative reading can enhance the generation of creative and experientially rich ideas, potentially leading to significant psychological and ecological benefits. The section discusses the potential qualities of imaginative reading, such as temporal regulation and resilience, in a rapidly evolving world, where shifting and global causes can be challenging to perceive, adapt to, and manage. It advocates for a revised focus in educational programs, emphasising the value of guided attention and habits shaped by awareness and training of multiscalar attention, pacemaking, and material engagement.

Overall, the Element introduces an overlooked perspective of how imaginative reading functions and how it should be taught. This new perspective is essential, as the dominant focus on reading has largely been confined to measuring efficiency and assessing outcomes such as cognitive and language skills and competencies, while neglecting the experiential and imaginative dimensions emerging *during* reading. Drawing on empirical examples, it explores how breaks in reading correlate with imaginative processes. Findings suggest that these breaks often emerge spontaneously rather than from deliberate reading strategies. Moreover, their occurrence and perceived value shift over time: while young readers naturally enjoy breaks, they gradually learn to suppress them rather than explore their potential. This trajectory suggests that normative approaches to reading instruction reinforce the perception of breaks as disruptions rather than opportunities for explorative engagement. By recognising the imaginative potential of breaks, we can shift the normative focus on breaks as negative towards their functionality, teaching readers to attend to them more intelligently and use them as a resource for imaginative thinking and agency. This reconceptualisation will not only enrich the reading experience but also cultivate broader cognitive and creative skills, ultimately contributing to more innovative and sustainable visions of the future.

1 Why Imagining? Why Reading?

If all the insects were to disappear from the earth, within 50 years all life on earth would end.

If all human beings disappeared from the earth, within 50 years all forms of life would flourish.

- Jonas Salk

1.1 Human Imagination and Trailblazing

Why is imagination important, and why must we understand this phenomenon? While humans may not hold a unique status in terms of planetary importance or significance, the undeniable reality lies in the myriad effects of human trailblazing: we make tracks and roads, produce artefacts such as literature and art, build institutions and cities, and drill mountains, manipulating the boundaries of places. While seas, mountains, weather, and fauna also impact the shape, direction, and quality of our future living, the human species currently has a direct and large-scale, unsustainable impact on our common future (Frank et al., 2024, Steffensen et al., 2024). For that reason, it is urgent to consider how human imagination and cognition, and the interactivity between human beings and their environment, can take on a sustainable form. Imagination is thus a human paradox: it has both created many of our problems and holds the potential to solve them (Graeber & Wengrow, 2021).

In this work, I do not aim to directly solve these problems. Instead, I propose focusing on how we can enhance sensitivity and awareness of emerging imaginative processes, which are crucial for critically engaging with the many local and global challenges we face. I believe that reading is one valuable practice, among others, for cultivating this imaginative capacity and awareness. In other words, it serves as a unique space for training attention to how one either opens up or closes down imaginative processes. Further, reading offers a safe haven to explore the impossible, allowing readers to imagine beyond conventional logic and functionalism. It opens a realm where ineffable, flickering experiences – such as the taste of sounds, transient emotions, and brief moments of simply being – can be embraced alongside grand ideas that challenge current ways of thinking and addressing crises. As readers navigate the words on a page, imagination transforms the act of reading into a dynamic, immersive experience (Ingold, 2022, 2024). This ludic dimension of human nature, where playfulness and creativity converge, could be more intelligently nurtured in our reading processes both in the flickering, rapid moment and within broader sustained engagements. By engaging our imaginative attitudes, we not only enrich our understanding and enjoyment of texts but also cultivate a mindset essential for empathetic connection in the face of contemporary challenges.

1.1.1 Where and What Is Imagination in the Current Scientific Landscape?

Despite the extensive body of research on imagination, a complete and unified definition and explanation of its nature remains elusive. This challenge arises from the non-localisable nature of the phenomenon, as there is no consistent correlation between the cognitive processes involved and their resultant effects, nor between the experiential processes and their biological substrates. While there is no imaginative organ buried in the neuroanatomical structures of the brain, many opposing candidates for its location have been suggested over time (Asma, 2017). Consequently, the diversity in theoretical frameworks and methodologies across disciplines further complicates the establishment of a comprehensive definition. There seems to be a consensus, however, on the uniqueness of the human mind's ability to generate novelties, with Darwin often cited as a reference: 'The imagination is one of the highest prerogatives of man. By this faculty he unites former images and ideas, independently of the will, and thus creates brilliant and novel results' (Darwin, 1871:45). Few question the existence of imagination; it seems almost instinctive to assume that it is there – part and parcel of the human mind. Further, by treating it as the mind's ability to generate novel ideas, experiences, or scenarios, it is typically anchored in mental imagery or symbolic thought.

Another discussion concerns the role and function of imagination. Scholars debate everything from its hierarchical structure and intentionality to the intertwined roles of the brain and body in imaginative processes. The strongest disagreements surface in fields like neuroscience and philosophy, including branches of phenomenology, where the mechanisms, origins, and even the very definition of imagination and its function remain points of contention (Asma, 2017). Neuroscience emphasises that imagination encompasses a wide array of mental activities that are not confined to specific neural pathways or regions, making it difficult to pinpoint a singular defining mechanism. Instead, it examines the complex workings of the brain to understand imagination, highlighting neural mechanisms and processes that enable mental imagery and creative thought, very much in line with Darwin's proposal. For instance, the neuroscientist, Stanislas Dehaene, studying the reading brain argues that '*imagination* ... enriches perception and, coupled to reason, can conceive new ways to achieve a goal' (Dehaene, 2009:321). This enriched perception invites novelty and is closely tied to creativity, as well as the ability to perceive beyond what is immediately present. At the core of this idea is the study of how the brain generates and manipulates mental images, involving key regions like the occipital lobe for visual processing and the prefrontal cortex for higher-order cognitive functions (Dehaene, 2009). The brain's default mode network (DMN), including the medial prefrontal cortex and posterior cingulate cortex, plays a crucial role, remaining active during rest and mind-wandering, facilitating imaginative tasks (Buckner, 2010; Buckner & Carroll, 2006; Buckner et al., 2008; Christoff et al., 2016; Hassabis & Maguire, 2009; Hassabis et al., 2007). Furthermore, using functional neuroimaging techniques such as fMRI and PET scans, neuroscientists visualise brain activity, pinpointing areas activated during the creation of new scenarios or the visualisation of past experiences (Christoff et al., 2009; Mason et al., 2007). Memory and learning are suggested to be intertwined with imagination, as the hippocampus helps recombine elements of past experiences to envision future events or novel ideas (Buckner & Carroll, 2006; Schacter et al., 2007). Thus, research in cognitive neuroscience suggests that memory retrieval and imaginative simulation share overlapping neural mechanisms, particularly within the DMN, reinforcing the idea that imagination is not merely a creative abstraction, but also a cognitive process grounded in memory reconstruction. Today, neuroplasticity, a modern term used to describe the brain's ability to form new neural connections, underpins the adaptability and growth of imaginative capabilities (Anderson, 2014; Dehaene, 2009). Furthermore, neurotransmitters like dopamine and serotonin are claimed to modulate mood, motivation, and creativity essential for imaginative thinking (Flaherty, 2005; Zabelina & Robinson, 2010). Lastly, developmental neuroscience sheds light on how imaginative abilities evolve across different life stages. Children's brains exhibit high plasticity, fostering rich imaginative play, while aging-related changes in neural connectivity may influence creative capacities over time (Thompson-Schill et al., 2009).

Philosophical discussions, on the contrary, are sometimes concerned with conceptual questions, diverting attention from the actual human behaviours we associate with the concept in the first place. In certain branches of analytical philosophy, as Stephen Asma argues, there is a tendency to over-intellectualise imagination, treating it as a mental mediator between particular sensations and conceptual universals. This view treats imagination merely as a byproduct of cognition, rather than as an embodied and dynamic process (Asma, 2017:4). Between the brain-centred approach in neuroscience and the highly conceptual tendencies in branches of analytical philosophy, there is a productive middle ground where phenomenological and ecological approaches to imagination are gaining traction. A whole array of disciplines that assume that cognition is embodied share key features in their work.

Presently, the interdisciplinary study of imagination integrates findings from neuroscience, psychology, philosophy, anthropology, and other fields, aiming for a more comprehensive understanding that respects both systematic observations and particular lived experiences (Asma, 2017; Ingold, 2022; van Dijk & Rietveld, 2020). Regardless of ongoing inconsistencies, there is broad agreement on imagination's multifaceted function: its creative and exploratory nature enhances learning experiences and contributes to intellectual development. Imagination is thus best understood as a cluster of processes that involve the whole body, integrating multiple timescales – past experiences, current material situations, and possible futures – leading to unpredictable and qualitatively diverse scenarios in action. These interwoven immaterial-material and perceptual-experiential dimensions make imagination challenging to categorise and study. While, like all cognitive processes, it unfolds within an ecological system and adheres to the fundamental constraints of physics, its emergent, dynamic, and context-dependent nature cannot be explained in purely physical terms. Thus, the study of imagination has a strong interdisciplinary appeal, captivating researchers due to its multifaceted role in human cognition, encompassing creativity, problem-solving, emotional engagement, cultural expression, entertainment, social understanding, and its profound impact on learning and intellectual pursuits.

The attempt here has not been to review the entire body of imagination literature, but rather to highlight the complexity of imagination's scientific status. For extensive discussions of imagination research, I refer to Asma, (2017), van Dijk & Rietveld (2020), and Forgeard & Kaufman (2015). For the purpose of this Element, I present in next section an ecological-embodied perspective on imagination that has been gaining ground over the last couple of decades.

1.1.2 An Ecological-Embodied Account of Imagining

One of the most comprehensive recent works on imagining is Ingold's (2022) book *Imagining for Real*. He is heavily influenced by James Gibson, an ecological psychologist who emphasised 'direct perception' (Gibson, 1979), a value-laden approach to visual perception. Gibson defines visual perception as a mechanism of 'the eyes in the head on a body supported by the ground' (Gibson, 1979:1) for detecting invariant structures in the environment. However, these structures are not passively perceived and then interpreted – they are directly picked up and understood as we move around in the environment. To explain this, Gibson introduces the concept of 'affordances': we do not perceive the environment as static collections of neutral information; rather, we perceive what it affords – its value and potential for action in relation to the perceiver. If affordances are perceived directly, then perception inherently involves an experiential dimension – it is not just about recognising structures but about grasping their value in relation to lived experience and needs. Crucially, for Gibson, both how we perceive (the mechanisms) and what we visually perceive (the structure in the ambient optic array) are universal. What changes is our experience of this structure over time, as it is shaped by ontogenetic and developmental processes from continuous interaction with the environment (Gibson, 1979; Heft, 2020).

Ingold argues that imagination does not emerge as a conscious choice but is instead an intrinsic species-specific attribute. An attribute that demands deeper understanding and more intelligent application. While he treats imagination as an essential aspect of human existence and creation, it is mistaken to reserve it solely for the pleasure of fantasy and fiction, a special form of thinking that is somehow loosely related to the environment. He advocates for an ecological account that links imagining directly to the environment, making it much closer to human perception in general, that is, as a way of envisioning a way forward. By this, he means that we perceive the environment not through the power of mental representations but 'by balancing one's very being on the cusp of its emergence' (Ingold, 2022:4). According to Ingold, imagining mostly joins with the world in that it contributes to what an individual can and would do next or next after the next. A person does not first look, then imagine, then feel – she perceives at once what is there, was there, or what was hoped to be there. Creation and creativity become closely aligned in this view, emerging from the integration of experience, desires, and needs with what the environment affords (cf. Rietveld, 2022; Kieverstein & Rietveld, 2020; Hodges & Baron, 1992). That is, we integrate the past into the present, making experience and imagination intrinsic to perception. As perception itself is direct, what we attend is shaped by bodily movement, expectations, and prior experience. This ensures that perception remains attuned to reality while also being selective and context-dependent (Goodwin, 1994). Yet, if we adopt an ecological approach, rejecting the idea of internal mental representations in general, then we must ask: where do we locate experience, thought, language, reflection, and imagination? In other words, what structures afford the emergence of the intangible, and can it be perceived? The deeper question, then, is whether imagination constitutes a distinct cognitive process, related, for instance, to conceptual thinking, or whether it is simply another, extended facet of perception, akin to imagery observation, shaped by the same mechanisms that govern our engagement with the ecological environment? This notion invites us to consider whether such immaterial structures can be perceived through similar mechanisms as material ones. Consider key cases of imagining; does listening to silent voices (such as inner speech or auditory verbal imagery) or visualising an imaginary firestorm rely on the same perceptual mechanisms that allow us to perceive temporary and quasi-stable phenomena such as structural variation in speech patterns, or persistent, stable objects such as books and pens? Further, does Gibson's suggestion of clear distinct ontological differences between material and immaterial information necessarily entail corresponding epistemological distinctions to the extent that one (the material) is defined as real and perception and the other (the immaterial) as unreal and imagination, implying two distinct cognitive functions (Gibson, 1979:256)? Or should they instead be understood as an immaterial-material continuum of perception?

I acknowledge that ontological distinctions can be crucial in determining the validity of certain experiences – such as whether one is perceiving a firestorm or hallucinating one. However, hallucinations are real hallucinations and carry tangible consequences for the perceiver, even if they do not hold intersubjective, empirical status. My focus, therefore, is not primarily on reality verification in the strict physical sense, but rather on the processes that enable perception and imagination as part of human life and experience. This perspective allows for a conception of reality that integrates metaphysical and physical dimensions, without collapsing all experiential processes into a single empirical or testable framework.

This extended approach to perception is crucial if we want to enhance imaginative capacities, which I argue can be developed by training attentional sensitivity – not only to the tangible but also to the intangible. Specifically, I am interested in how these processes allow readers to explore facets of their potentialities and how attentional sensitivity and imaginative capacity can be intrinsically linked through training. If perception and imagination share a fundamental basis, then what we call immaterial may not belong to a separate domain but rather constitute an extended or multi-layered dimension of our informational field. In this view, the immaterial is not a distinct cognitive function but instead an expansion and extension of perception, operating within the same embodied dynamics that structure our engagement with the ecological environment.

Gibson, too, remains cautious about these distinctions, suggesting that while processes such as imagining and daydreaming are unreal and not 'strictly perceptual', they still depend on the visual system, as we have learned to abstract invariants across contexts: 'a perceptual system that has become sensitized to certain invariants and can extract them from the stimulus flux can also operate without the constraints of the stimulus flux. Information becomes further detached from stimulation. The adjustment loops for looking around, looking at, scanning, and focusing are then inoperative. The visual system visualizes. But this is still an activity of the system, not an appearance in the theatre of consciousness' (Gibson, 1979:256).

Thus, imagining is not separate from perceiving; rather, it is perceiving more broadly. *Visual* perception, in its strictest technical sense – central to Gibson's project – relies on detecting real invariant structures by moving around in an ecological human-scale environment. I acknowledge that my project extends beyond Gibson's localised focus on what is tangible, available in its persistent qualities and as such can be detected by the visual system in real time. Notice that I do not suggest that we *directly* perceive processes such as the erosion of a mountain or the movement of electrons in atoms as they occur at timescales and spatial resolutions beyond human direct perceptual capacities (cf. Gibson, 1979:12 [italic in the original]). Also, while we perceive the sun as going down, we know that it is the Earth that is turning. This knowledge affects our experience but does not alter our perception – perceptually, the sun appears to set because it is gradually occluded by the horizon, and visual occlusion specifies that one object is moving behind another (Heft, 2020). However, my point is that we *can* perceive such processes indirectly using imaginative capacities, drawing on similar mechanisms to those involved in detecting invariant structures in ecological perception. This ability relies on experience – as does all socially constituted or knowledgeable perception – with using tools, models, and instruments that allow us to visualise different perspectives such as seeing the world from the atmosphere.

In other words, the same cognitive and perceptual principles that allow us to perceive environmental structure directly also enable us to detect phenomena indirectly, as I also touched upon in the introduction. While some conceptual processes might be entirely distinct from perception, my focus is on integrating those that share key features with perception, enabling a kind of double perception (cf. Gibson, 1979:283). This entails simultaneously engaging with both material and immaterial structures, as seen in reading, where one perceives written marks while also perceiving meaning beyond their physical structures (cf. Section 1.2.3). Such a perspective broadens the scope of perception by encompassing not only the directly visually perceivable environment but also what lies beyond our immediate sensory reach. This expanded view of perception accounts for more than just what is materially present. It includes the ability to perceive absence: what once was but is no longer, what could have been, or what was anticipated but never materialised.

Imagination is the human way of engaging with the world in its local and non-local forms. An engagement that emerges from the fact that we are living beings always shaped by our experiences (linguistic, cultural, etc.) and emerging circumstances. As stated in the introduction, 'the imagination pulse' serves as a metaphor for capturing the varying degrees of imagination, pulsating in every beat of our bodies, and as an intrinsic aspect of our existence. As such it can be foregrounded or relegated depending on expertise, task, and circumstance, but like our pulse, it is always with us. Just as our pulse can change significantly in a split second, that will draw our attention to it, imagination can also shift from a background presence to a vivid force, directing our engagement with the world in new ways. Imagination allows humans to act as active conductors of temporal integration, leading to creative processes and outcomes like playing and producing music, creating art, making products, building cities, and inventing technological solutions (for good and for ill). It thus emerges on a continuum from flickers to firestorms both in terms of experience, process, outcome, and consequence. The crucial claim here is that we can learn to regulate the temporal dynamics guiding attention in ways that either speed up or slow down the imaginative processes, impacting the process, experience and outcome of the process itself. Temporal regulation of perception-action cycles is especially relevant in today's world, where the emphasis on outcomes and efficiency often sidelines imagining – particularly when it is slow, operates outside a functional framework, or remains in a latent, ineffable state.

The idea is that reading is an apt case (but not an exclusive one) for training imaginative processes through modulating engagement and attention. First, I discuss the problems of the current world's narrow focus on outcomes and efficiency for the imaginative potential in general, and why reading offers an antidote to this cultural and ecological condition, if understood in a less task-oriented way (cf. Trasmundi et al., 2024).

1.1.3 Imagination on a Continuum – Placing Ourselves at One End

Imagination holds the potential for profound aesthetic creation and transformative outcomes, yet it can also be commodified and risk devolving into predictability and triviality when constrained by instrumental frameworks. An increasing number of scholars express concern that human imagination and creativity are progressively constrained by the structures of modernity, with real and far-reaching consequences. Graeber & Wengrow (2021) argue that human imagination, particularly at a global scale, has become marked by a surprising lack of originality and boldness. They illustrate this point by highlighting the inability of contemporary societies to envision alternative ways of living, suggesting that rather than seeking fundamental change, humanity tends to make incremental adjustments or passively adhere to prevailing norms and technological advancements. At some point in human history, Graeber &

Wengrow suggest, we lost the capacity to imagine radically different forms of existence, becoming trapped in predictable patterns of thought. This challenge is historical, as they trace it through the human past and present. Their work underscores the global and temporal scale of this issue, contending that truly transformative actions are exceedingly rare today, whereas historically, such imaginative leaps were far more common:

> the evidence we have from Palaeolithic time onwards suggests that many – perhaps most – people did not merely imagine or enact different social orders at different times a year, but actually lived in them for extended periods of time. The contrast with our present situation could not be more stark. Nowadays, most of us find it increasingly difficult even to picture what an alternative economic or social order would be like. Our distant ancestors seem, by contrast, to have moved regularly back and forth between them. If something did go terribly wrong in human history – and given the current state of the world, it's hard to deny something did – then perhaps it began to go wrong precisely when people started losing that freedom to imagine and enact other forms of social existence, to such a degree that some now feel this particular type of freedom hardly even existed. (Graeber & Wengrow, 2021:502)

Other scholars propose that the loss of imaginative freedom coincided with a broader societal shift. They suggest that the loss of the freedom to imagine overlapped with a period when societal changes began to occur at a pace asynchronous with the scale of human ecological perception. As these processes became increasingly mechanised, opportunities for imagination and well-being were compromised. Amongst others, Hartmut Rosa (2020) emphasises the need for aesthetic, artistic, and temporal engagement as essential for fostering reflection, creativity, and well-being. He describes (post)modern society as dominated by accelerating social-material processes, which inhibit these fundamental capacities. According to Rosa, this acceleration turns growth and innovation from symbols of progress into claustrophobic forces that create existential anxiety (Rosa, 2020). This frenetic pace disrupts our ability to align with natural and socio-material rhythms, pushing individuals into a relentless cycle of productivity that diminishes time for meaningful engagement with the world, thereby limiting opportunities for the creative and reflective processes necessary for well-being. This acceleration conditions an aggressive relationship with the world, fostering a kind of engagement that leaves little time to synchronise with biological or cultural rhythms that deviate from the dominant pulse of productivity. On a large scale, the pace of society surpasses the individual's capacity to integrate these processes, resulting in widespread stress, anxiety, and related issues (Rosa, 2020). This accelerated societal pace also permeates educational practices, including reading, transforming it into an activity focused on 'how much' rather than 'how well', leaving little room for reflection (Collini, 2018; Ingold, 2024). In modern Western contexts, perception is further entangled with technological, digital, and industrial systems, rendering the underlying operations and their consequences opaque, disconnected from human experience.

Henri Lefebvre's critique of capitalist society resonates here too. He argues that modern capitalism imposes rhythms that are increasingly asynchronous with human bodily rhythms, resulting in pathological outcomes. Capitalism, Lefebvre argues, 'kills nature ... It kills creation, creative capacity. It goes as far as threatening the last resource: nature, the fatherland, roots. It delocalises humans' (Lefebvre, 2004:53).

According to Rosa, the only response to this trend is resilience in the form of embodied resonance. He characterises resonance by how a person is affected bodily, responds to this affectivity, feels transformed, and experiences a state of unpredictability emerging from bodily engagement with the environment (Rosa, 2020). As such, resonance starkly contrasts with modern society's focus on measurement, control, prediction, exploitation, and production. Rosa's resonance theory has often been applied to aesthetic and artistic processes, emphasising that creative and thoughtful engagement requires time and the space for reflection. However, I argue that this form of resilient behaviour should not be limited to specific artistic processes; rather, it must be integrated into the full range of everyday activities. In this regard, reading provides an exemplary case for practicing temporal regulation, offering a means to integrate resilient, reflective behaviour into daily life.

1.2 What Reading Practice Has Been, Is, and Can Become

1.2.1 The Landscape of Codes

What reading practice has been, what it is, and what it can become are points of inquiry that challenge not only historical perceptions of reading processes and function but also the very frameworks through which we engage with texts today.

The traditional view of reading, grounded in cognitive science and psychological models, often positions it as a linear, symbolic process, akin to encoding and decoding. The 'code view' of reading, as advanced by researchers such as Dehaene (2009), posits that reading involves the extraction of meaning from text through cognitive steps akin to computational processes. While this view has been useful in understanding the neurological underpinnings of reading, it fails to account for the full scope of what happens when we read in different contexts and how it shapes our experience. Dehaene himself acknowledges that despite progress in understanding the brain's role in reading, we remain far from explaining how meaning and imagination emerge from reading texts. For instance, he refers to the opening lines of Nabokov's novel, *Lolita,* as an example of how reading engages not only our cognitive faculties but also our aesthetic and bodily senses: 'Lolita, light of my life, fire of my loins. My sin, my soul. Lo-lee-ta: the tip of the tongue taking a trip of three steps down the palate to tap, at three, on the teeth. Lo. Lee. Ta'. (Dehaene, 2009:1). Reading this passage is not simply about decoding letters into sounds; it is an interwoven experience of aesthetic judgment, poetic style, and bodily sensation. The rhythm of the words and the physical movements they evoke in the reader's mouth create a bodily engagement with the text that goes beyond mere interpretation. That is, reading activates multiple muscles, even in silent reading, revealing the whole-bodied nature of the experience (Baron, 2021; Mangen & Schilhab, 2012; Wolf, 2018). Such embodied experiences in reading demonstrate the multiscalarity of the act. Imagination and meaning arise not from abstract decoding but from a rich, integrated experience that engages the body, the mind, and previous life experiences. Neuroscience struggles to explain how these complex imaginative universes are created through the act of reading. While Dehaene's (2009) work remains a landmark in understanding the neural basis of reading, more recent research has begun to explore the intricate interplay between reading, cognition, and imagination. For instance, Maryanne Wolf (2018) has argued that deep reading fosters cognitive flexibility, perspective-taking, and creative thought, highlighting the importance of reading as an immersive and reflective act rather than just a process of decoding symbols. Dehaene himself admits that neuroscience has only begun to scratch the surface of how meaning is constructed in the brain, and he basically suggests a list of hypotheses about what might happen:

> although researchers have managed to map several of the relevant brain areas, how meaning is actually coded into the cortex remains a frustrating issue. The processes that allow our neuronal networks to snap together and "make sense" remains utterly mysterious. We do not know, however, that meaning cannot be confined to only a few brain regions and probably depends on vast arrays of neurons distributed throughout the cortex, of which the frontal and temporal regions ... are just the tip of the iceberg. Although these regions activate when we access the gist of a word, they probably do not store the meaning itself, but merely facilitate access to semantic information spread out elsewhere in the cortex. According to the neurologist, Antonio Damasio, they may well operate as "convergence zones" that gather and send signals to many other regions. They thus, in all likelihood, collect dispersed fragments of meaning and bundle them together into articulated sets of neurons that constitute the genuine neuronal substrate of word meaning (Dehaene, 2009:111–112).

This admission underscores the limitations of cognitivist approaches to reading, particularly in capturing its imaginative and bodily experiential dimensions. While neuroscience has made significant strides in mapping the brain's involvement in reading as a process of pattern recognition, it cannot explain how reading functions as a whole-bodied, temporal, imaginative, and transformative process. Understanding reading in its fullest embodied-ecological sense requires an interdisciplinary approach – one that integrates cognitive science, anthropology, and ecological-embodied perspectives to account for the richness of literary experience beyond neural mechanisms alone.

Ingold criticises psychology's view on reading:

> To regard reading as a decoding operation, converting a sequence of letters into a corresponding series of sounds, is to start from an absurdly narrow base – so narrow, indeed, that it includes barely a fraction of what people actually do when they read (even assuming that they use an alphabetic script), while at the same time putting it easily within range of a relatively simple machine intelligence (Ingold, 2024:1).

His critique stems from the longstanding view on reading in psychology that ignores its historical roots. And he continues his critique: 'we have indeed forgotten what it means truly to inhabit the page, and our theories of reading reflect this. We could not otherwise even imagine that reading is a simple operation of decoding. Is it too much to ask of psychology that it should desist from projecting its amnesia towards the past into its designs for the intelligence of the future?' (Ingold, 2024:7). His own response to this critique begins with a historical awareness of how reading originally held a meaning quite different from the modern conception – an understanding he believes is crucial for addressing reading education and practices intelligently today.

1.2.2 What an Anthropology of Reading Teaches Us

Ingold's anthropological approach to reading challenges the idea that reading is a fixed, uniform practice across time. Instead, he argues that reading habits have evolved alongside societal changes, shaped by historical, cultural, and technological influences. For instance, the shift from oral to silent reading in the late Middle Ages, facilitated by innovations like the use of spaces between words (introduced by Irish scribes in the seventh century), marked a significant transformation in how people engaged with texts. Punctuation enabled readers to anticipate and comprehend texts more rapidly, laying the groundwork for modern silent reading practices (Kristiansen et al., 2024; Manguel, 2014).

The evolution of reading in the sixteenth century saw further changes, influenced by figures like Martin Luther, who advocated for a more scientific, analytical approach to texts. This shift marked a departure from earlier medieval practices where manuscripts were often left open, inviting readers to engage with them in creative and interactive ways. Readers would annotate the margins, make notes between the lines, and revisit passages, but with the advent of the bound book, these interactive practices were gradually replaced by a more linear, closed form of reading (Ingold, 2022; Kristiansen et al., 2024).

This transformation mirrored broader intellectual trends, notably Bacon's rise of empiricism, which encouraged a literal, analytical reading of nature, stripped of imaginative interpretation. Nature, once seen as a creative, autobiographical text, became more of a mathematical substrate, devoid of the author's direct creative influence. This shift from creative to analytical modes of thinking also impacted how reading was conceptualised. The emergence of the 'code view' of reading further develops this notion by framing reading primarily as a cognitive task of symbol decoding, rather than as an activity that encourages imaginative engagement. This perspective reduces reading to mechanical processing of linguistic signs, overlooking the creative dimensions involved in immersive, deep, and reflective reading (cf. Ingold, 2022; Cobley & Siebers, 2021).

However, as mentioned in the introduction, contemporary empirical research in embodied cognition has begun to challenge this view, offering a 4E cognition framework for understanding reading as an embodied, enactive, embedded, and extended process (Gallagher, 2018; Kukkonen, 2020; Mangen & Schilhab, 2012). In the context of reading, this framework shifts the focus from mental representations to the reader's bodily engagement with text. Research by Mangen and colleagues (Mangen, 2008, 2016; Mangen & Schilhab, 2012; Mangen et al., 2019; Trasmundi et al., 2021) has demonstrated how tactile feedback, the movement of the hands, and the physicality of the reading medium all play a crucial role in shaping the reading experience. Yet, even within these frameworks, the focus often remains on task-oriented goals such as comprehension and fluency, overlooking the ruptures and pauses that occur during reading. The task-based epistemology underlying psychological and educational models of reading fails to account for the moments of imaginative engagement that disrupt the flow of reading (Trasmundi et al., 2024).

1.2.3 An Ecological-Embodied Approach to Reading

Drawing on principles from ecological psychology and 4E cognitive science, I explore reading as a social, whole-bodied engagement with a material object and its symbolic landscape (Cobley & Siebers, 2021; Trasmundi & Cowley, 2020; Trasmundi et al., 2024). Ecological psychology and 4E cognitive science have traditionally excelled in explaining the technical mechanics and systemic coordination dynamics underlying perception, navigation, and behaviour; focusing on how a person looks up, moves, makes decisions, and solves problems within their environment. Furthermore, while these approaches have been considerably applied to language and interaction studies (Baggs, 2021; Bruineberg & Van den Herik, 2021; Hutchins, 2013; Malafouris, 2013; McClelland, 2020; Steffensen et al., 2024; Trasmundi, 2020), their application to expert reading remains underdeveloped within this framework. This may be because higher-order processes were not the original focus of Gibson's project, leaving a significant amount of conceptual and empirical work to be done in these fields.

Gibson himself was clear about the scope and rigorous focus of his project. In his 1979 *Magnum Opus,* he explicitly states that he is less concerned with higher-order processes central to the argument presented in this book:

> The explanation of how we human observers ... can *visualize* an atom or a galaxy even if we cannot *see* one, will not be attempted at this stage of the inquiry. ... We must first consider how we can perceive the environment–how we apprehend the same things that our human ancestors did before they learned about atoms and galaxies. We are concerned with direct perception, not so much with the indirect perception got by using microscopes ... and pictures, still less with the kind of apprehension got by speech and writing (Gibson, 1979:10 [italic in the original]).

Naturally, this is where my project extends beyond Gibson's focus: I aim to understand how a cultural being perceives material-symbolic artefacts as part of a broader social practice – one in which she is aware of atoms and galaxies and engages with speech and culturally embedded activities such as reading.

After all, reading is not fundamentally different from the way we perceive atoms and galaxies or use language to extend perception beyond immediate sensory input (Steffensen et al., 2024).

While visual perception is confined to what we see by moving in our environment, multimodal, or embodied perception extends far beyond the visual domain. This broader perceptual framework allows phenomena such as 'social practices' to gain an empirical grounding through an embodied history of guided attention to multi-layered information. The perception of social phenomena requires an active and continuous effort to attune to multiple, nested, and complex informational structures, such as those embedded in language, emotions, behaviours, and events – enabling us to grasp their significance beyond their real-time configuration. For instance, as a literate person, I do not merely perceive isolated objects or books such as a person, a text, and a gaze, rather, I perceive *a reading practice*. That is, I perceive holistically, integrating clusters of nested, discrete information including the complex *relations* between informational structures. This comprised perception relates to the function of affordances, because perceiving an affordance is more efficient than processing all individual variables separately. Rather than requiring complete information, we only need sufficient data to guide action and maintain forward movement. Gibson elaborates: 'an affordance is an invariant combination of variables, and one might guess that it is easier to perceive such an invariant unit than it is to perceive all the variables separately. It is never necessary to distinguish *all* the features of an object and, in fact, it would be impossible to do so. Perception is economical' (Gibson, 1979:134–135).

Unlike direct perception of the unmediated environment, reading introduces an additional layer: the mediation of symbols that requires an imaginative extension of perception. This idea aligns with theories of perceptual social learning, where repeated and guided exposure to structured invariants enhances attention and expertise (Gibson, 1965; Goodwin, 1994; Gibson, 1979). Over time a reader becomes increasingly skilled in merging direct and indirect perception. 'Perceiving gets wider and finer and longer and richer and fuller ... Note how this definition includes within perception a part of memory, expectation, knowledge, and meaning–some part but not all of those processes in each case' (Gibson, 1979:255). Used in the context of reading, this means that, a reader does not only perceive the letters 'f-i-r-e-s-t-o-r-m', or the word 'firestorm' but can also at the same time visualise aspects of a firestorm or completely different associations. However, the richness of the visualisation, might fluctuate over the course of reading. When significantly elaborate and vivid it can influence the reading process, potentially slowing down patterned symbol recognition as attention is distributed across multiple timescales. This perspective on reading presents an untapped potential for exploring how self-elicited breaks shape imaginative engagement by fostering attentional shifts and awareness of pacemaking strategies. The interplay between structured information and imaginative expansion transforms reading into a dynamically unfolding experience, where meaning is continuously shaped through the interaction of perception and cognition.

While each person perceives the environment in a unique way – due *not* to abstract cognitive systems, but to their distinct lived history and bodily design – there are also shared aspects of perception, as humans inhabit a common social world (Heft, 2020; Hodges & Baron, 1992: Jensen & Pedersen, 2016). Temporal integration of lived experience, including norms and rules, and situational circumstances, is essential for constructing a coherent narrative of self and environment, enabling complex cognitive functions such as reading (Trasmundi, 2025). The ability to perceive events as part of broader narratives enables socialisation. Gibson points out: 'the child begins by perceiving the affordances of things for her own personal behaviour. But she must learn to perceive the affordances of things for other observers as well. Only when each child perceives the value of things for others does she begin to be socialized' (Gibson, 1979:141). Social affordances thus emerge from an individual's lived history of social encounters and practices, continuously and dynamically shaping and guiding attentional sensitivity as they engage with and navigate persistent social and material environments (Baggs, 2021; Kyselo, 2023). Reading, as a manifestation of engagement over time, builds on these foundations, integrating attention, embodied experience, and knowledge reconfiguration to engage with written language in ways that extend beyond the immediate perception of structured marks on a page (Ingold, 2022). It is a social and personal activity at once, just as it is perceptual and imaginative at once.

Overall, the letters on the page, shaped by norms and conventions of writing systems, both constrain and liberate this imaginative engagement. The act of reading modern, alphabetic texts reflects a complex interplay of biological, cultural, and technological influences, each shaping human cognition in distinct ways. However, to appreciate the depth of imaginative reading, we must consider the critical role that breaks play in the flow of this process. That is the topic of the following section.

2 Breaks and Their Role in Imaginative Reading

> Thinking begins with in what may fairly enough be called a forkedroad situation, a situation which is ambiguous, which presents a dilemma, which proposes alternatives. As long as our activity glides smoothly along from one thing to another, or as long as we permit our **imagination** to entertain fancies at pleasure, there is no call for reflection. **Difficulty or obstruction in the way of reaching a belief brings us, however, to a pause.** ... Demand for the solution of a perplexity is the steadying and guiding factor in the entire process of reflection. Where there is no question of a problem to be solved or a difficulty to be surmounted, the course of suggestions flows on at random ... Thinking is not a case of spontaneous combustion; it does not occur on "general principles." There is something specific which occasions and evokes it. ... **Reflective thinking, in short, means judgement suspended during further inquiry; and suspense is likely to be somewhat painful.**
>   - my emphasis, Dewey, 1910:11ff. [bold added for emphasis].

2.1 Why Are Breaks Crucial in Reading, and Why Does No One Study Them?

Consider the simple question: What characterises your own reading? To answer that question, you will need to consider an array of activities that go on as you engage with written material. For instance, imagine every rapid embodied adjustment and gesture your body makes: how you speed up or slow down;

imagine your eyes' rapid saccading or how you look up and away from the page, how you impose rhythmicality, stop, continue, go back, make connections, and free associations, how you leaf through passages, point to the material, put it down or closer to you, how you underline, sigh, laugh, and generally experience emotional responses which consist of much more than the linguistic meaning of the words you read. You constantly make embodied-affective judgements (Benne, 2021; Macrine & Fugate, 2022; Trasmundi et al., 2022). That is, your reading involves multiple ripples and breaks. Yet, surprisingly, the significance of these micro-breaks has not been thoroughly described in reading research.

Conceptually, a break is a change in a pattern; a punctuation of equilibrium (Stewart, 2019). In an ecological-embodied framework, perception remains continuous, but experience is modulated through attentional shifts. Breaks in reading, therefore, do not 'alter' perception itself but instead recalibrate how we attend to and experience the text's affordances. A break is *not* necessarily a halt or a breakdown. Rather, a break simply disrupts the pattern in ways that alter the anticipation of the next moment. It is an opening. Empirically, it can be identified as a shift in attention or behaviour that impacts the overall flow of ongoing events. To integrate breaks as part and parcel of imaginative reading, a new conceptual-empirical framework of reading is required. This integration highlights temporal modulations in reading and allows for a systematic testing of their nature in terms of conditions and significance, enriching our understanding of how they might relate to the richness of imaginative processes. The radical view here is that what appears to be task-switching, lack of concentration, or breakdowns are instead key for exploring imaginative reading. It involves temporal loopholes or painful suspense in Dewey's terms above. These moments not only welcome reflection but also foster a dynamic style of attending in reading. This idea aligns with research on perceptual sensitivity, where skilled individuals refine their ability to detect subtle patterns in dynamic environments (Gibson, 1979; Goodwin, 1994). Just as an experienced tracker perceives meaningful signs in a landscape or a musician anticipates tonal shifts, breaks in reading allow for a recalibration of focus and thinking. While reading is indeed a socio-cultural practice, it is also a personal and subjective activity as it integrates lived experience, habits of attending, and bodily resources altogether, creating a unique and personal reading style. How readers engage with breaks depends on their experience, culture, skill, and circumstances.

Dewey (2010) suggested that breaks are understood as forked-road situations, saturated with ambiguity. If these moments are imbued with suspense, rich imagination, and critical reflection, there is potential in empirically exploring the conditions that foster their emergence. Developing a sensitivity to these conditions could lead to experiencing many more processes as forked-road situations. This heightened awareness also sharpens attention to rapid changes, allowing the reader to experience subtle nuances and curiosities that might otherwise go unnoticed.

This idea, that breaks fuel the imagination, is not new. In fact, it was proposed over half a millennium ago in the Japanese tradition of Noh theatre. I will devote some space to describe this ancient tradition and explore how the concepts of waiting, hesitating, enduring, and pausing can enrich our understanding of imagination in the context of reading.

2.2 Japanese Philosophy and Dramaturgy of Temporality in the Noh Theatre

An important theoretical backbone that gives flesh to the Element's argument about imagination and breaks is the theory and dramaturgy of 'living pauses' from the Japanese Noh theatre established by Zeami in the fourteenth to fifteenth centuries. Zeami, the greatest playwright and theorist of the Japanese Noh theatre, contributed to one of the oldest forms of traditional Japanese drama, a testimony to the enduring power of minimalist performance. Noh artfully blends dance, drama, music, and poetry into an integrated aesthetic experience. Its historical roots stretch deep into Japanese culture, and its influence continues to resonate today (Kono, 2022; Moriooka, 2015).

The essence of Noh lies in its minimalism and symbolism. The stage is an unadorned wooden platform, focusing the audience's attention to the actors' movements and vocalising. See Figure 1 for an overview of the Noh stage.

Every gesture of the performer carries a symbolic meaning, as does its timing and duration. This strong simplicity allows for rich emotional and spiritual

Figure 1 Key components of Noh Theatre, highlighting the minimalist aesthetics, rooted in Japanese classical traditions

narratives, further reckoned in the decoration and use of masks and costumes. Crafted from wood, the masks represent a myriad of characters, emotions, and states of being. Each mask is a work of art, transforming the actor into their character, and adding layers of depth to the performance. To understand the values of a Noh performance requires high-cultural knowledge.

Consider the resemblance with modern reading: A book, like a Noh stage, carries symbolic traces, such as a book cover, pages, and the written or printed word. Just as an audience interprets Noh through their own unique perspective informed by cultural understanding, a reader engages with a text from their subjective position within a broader cultural context.

The slow, deliberate pacing in Noh, known as 'Jo-ha-kyu', creates a rhythmic ebb and flow similar to breathing, allowing the audience to become immersed in the performance.[1] These subtle gestures hold profound significance, much like the rhythms readers create during puzzling moments. Also, music and chanting play a crucial role in Noh with a small ensemble of musicians providing the accompaniment. Traditional Japanese instruments such as the flute and drums set the tone, enhancing the emotional and spiritual style of the performance. At the narrative level, there are central themes being explored in Noh's plays which pivot around integrated concepts spanning spirituality, the supernatural, and the human condition. Stories drawn from Japanese literature, history, and folklore feature prominently, with characters that include ghosts, gods, and legendary heroes. These narratives are not just tales; they are explorations of profound philosophical and existential questions. A Noh performance is therefore more than an entertainment event or a window into a cultural practice; rather, it is described by practitioners of Noh, experts, and historians as an experience that resonates with Japanese lifeforms at a very general level (Kono, 2022; Moriooka, 2015).

Particular concepts are pivotal for Japanese lifeforms. Among the Japanese terms adopted into English is 間 'ma', meaning *interval between things* or *space in between* or *a gap/pause*. The interpretation of 'ma' varies based on context, highlighting the interplay between elements (awai), the spatial gap between objects (aida), or the relational distance between individuals (aidagara). In Noh, ma emphasises the importance of a living pause; a form of bodily tension and silence allowing the audience moments of reflection and engagement with the performance. This use of space and stillness is what sets Noh apart, creating a meditative atmosphere that contrasts sharply with the fast-paced, visually overloaded nature of much contemporary entertainment. In the context of

---

[1] https://deeperjapan.com/journal/experiencing-time-through-the-lens-of-jo-ha-ky.

reading, 'ma' can be understood as the space between moments of engagement – a threshold where imaginative processes deepen. Just as the Noh performer's deliberate pause heightens the audience's anticipation and reflection, reading breaks function as spaces where meaning expands beyond immediate comprehension (Kukkonen, 2020). The tension, emerging during a Noh pause, is not an absence but an active structuring of attention, much like the dynamic interplay between silence and sound in music. This principle applies to reading, where pauses enable a richer form of imagining.

Another Japanese concept closely related to ma is 'senu-hima' (閑暇) meaning *a moment of nothing* (Kono, 2022; Moriooka, 2015). The term embodies the idea of deliberate pauses or moments of non-action, often translated as 'leisure' or 'free time'. The kanji characters for Senu Hima are 閑 (sen) and 暇 (hima). 閑 (sen) represents tranquility or quietness, often depicting a state of calm or inactivity. It conveys a sense of peace and deliberate stillness. 暇 (hima) signifies free time or leisure, implying a period when one is not occupied with work or specific duties. Combined, 閑暇 (senu hima) reflects the cultural value placed on taking breaks and allowing space for reflection and rejuvenation. It suggests that these moments of inactivity are charged with potential for cognitive and emotional reconstruction. This concept aligns with traditional Japanese aesthetics, emphasising the importance of pauses and intervals in creating a harmonious and fulfilling life.

To understand the empirical dynamics of these concepts, the Japanese Noh theatre employs ma and senu-hima through sudden breaks in their smooth and significant pacing across the stage. This involves: 'taking a pause, maintaining silence, and in experiencing the deepened chronotope' (Moriooka, 2015:14). The concept gives weight to the idea that breaks are not just empty voids but meaningful because of their transition potential. In Noh theatre, the moment of no-action (senu-hima), which includes ma, connects one motion to the next. Ma is 'giving space for inner recapitulation, rehearsal, and imagination [and] is a facilitating factor in dialogical relationships' (Hermans & Hermans-Konopka 2010:294). Ma is further described as a basic phenomenon of controlled action-perception and defined as crucial for generating quality in life, rich imagination, and dialogical skills (Moriooka, 2015). Further, breaks in the Noh theatre have been described as the most intriguing moments because they disturb anticipation, habitual thinking, and prediction. When flow is broken, the break constitutes a threshold for new beginnings. A break during an activity can be an imaginative incubation phase where everything becomes possible. When the Noh-performer suddenly freezes on the stage, the audiences hold their breaths, are highly alert, and cognitive-affectively engaged (Moriooka, 2015). The tension is not at all speculative or metaphysical; rather, it is felt and observable: 'The actor's internal mindful effort is critical. Superficially, it may seem that the actor has halted his movement; however, his inner tension must be maintained' (Moriooka, 2015:90). This control of attention is similar to breaks in reading because the reader allows associative ways of thinking to percolate without losing track of the overall project (Linell, 2009). When the narrative unfolding is momentarily disrupted, the rhythmic break serves as an imaginative opening where past experiences, present interpretations, and future anticipations interact. In reading, such pauses afford opportunities for readers to reorient, project possibilities, and enrich their engagement.

In reading, this means that ma can be treated as an immanent gap. It cannot be located a priori, as it is relational in nature. It emerges depending on the preceding and subsequent patterns. For instance, ma can be experienced in the gaps between chapters, pages, and words. Ma can also exist within a word or a sound, as will be demonstrated in the following section. It basically refers to the local break within a global pattern, such as patterns of sound, movement, and form. To uphold an event or task where breaks are rich and multiple requires an alert and attentive attitude.

The link between a Japanese philosophy of temporality and an ecological-embodied framework begins to crystalise. An embodied understanding of imagining can expand the notion of the 'inner' tension to a bodily observed phenomenon. Or put differently, senu-hima is not just an inner tension but also an embodied performance that in the Noh-theatre is described as kami (the performance of the sound of silence). It indicates how the performers hold their breaths for a while, and that performance will determine every action that follows in terms of strength, pitch, speed, and timing. It seems inevitable to investigate breaks in reading too. And further to explore how ma can be applied to the case of reading and to education and learning more generally. A break is an observable, empirical, interdisciplinary starting point for opening up new questions about the complexity of reading in relation to imagination.

Noh teaches us that sometimes less is more; that through minimalism and careful attention to detail, profound beauty and meaning can emerge. It invites us to slow down, to pay attention, and to find resonance in the spaces in-between. This philosophy becomes a resonance to the accelerations that otherwise saturate our modern modes of existence. Just as Noh theatre draws its audience into a contemplative state, so too can reading, when approached with a similar mindfulness. It can become an immersive and transformative experience where the reader becomes skilled in modulating reading pace. I suggest combining the idea of breaks with the ecological-embodied framework to imaginative reading to generate the defining properties of a theory of imaginative reading. Let us explore these properties further.

2.3 The Defining Properties in a Theory of Imaginative Reading

The core argument of this Element is that breaks play a crucial role in rich imagining during reading. While other aspects of reading are certainly important, this Element focuses exclusively on breaks, as they have been largely overlooked in previous research. I will therefore suggest focusing on three defining properties of a theory of imaginative reading, namely: (i) multiscalar attention, (ii) pacemaking, and (iii) material engagement.

In practice, each dimension is interconnected with the others and cannot be understood in isolation. However, I will introduce each separately and then demonstrate how focusing on their integration puts our understanding of reading in a new light. These dimensions are present in all forms of reading, but by focusing on them, we can reframe our view of reading as a dynamic, imaginative process by recognising how attention, rhythm, and material engagement shape and condition breaks. Further, we can use this knowledge to cultivate specific reading strategies that enhance imaginative reading.

- **Multiscalar attention**
  Imaginative reading transcends basic linguistic comprehension by connecting experiences across multiple timescales – past, present, and future – allowing the reader to engage in complex thought patterns that integrate textual reading with a reader's hope, expectations and values. This integration fosters novel connections and ideas. Breaks are essential for modulating attention, allowing readers to shift focus across different scales and challenging the conventional real-time, code-based model of reading. Drawing on ecological theories of action-perception, multiscalar attention makes breaks not just interruptions but productive moments for imaginative engagement, enabling dynamic shifts and integration of multiple attention points in and beyond the textual surface.

- **Pacemaking**
  By modulating reading rhythm, readers create opportunities for imaginative engagement – whether through brief adjustments or extended reflection. When applied deliberately, these changes in pace allow for intelligent exploratory and dynamic reading experience, making space for both imaginative flickers and firestorms in reading. Drawing on concepts from Japanese dramaturgy, pacemaking turns these shifts into creative openings, revealing new layers of understanding and engagement.

- **Material engagement**
  Imaginative reading is a whole-bodied experience that involves direct interaction with the physical text in a context. Material engagement extends beyond visual or linguistic processing, incorporating tactile, auditory, and spatial elements that shape reading habits and expertise. Material engagement

theory reveals how breaks in reading can enhance cognitive and imaginative potential by leveraging this dynamic interaction between mind and material.

Let us elaborate on the three dimensions further.

Multiscalar attention in reading, from an ecological-embodied perspective, is not only about drawing on multiple sensory modalities in the present moment. It also emphasises the interconnected habits that enable readers to engage in cultural practices rooted in writing systems and language. Skilled linguistic action allows readers not only to understand text but also to reconstruct and re-evoke personal life experiences in response to the symbols encountered (Cowley, 2021). Reading is thus a multiscalar activity, where the present moment of engagement with a text is enriched by past experiences, cultural practices, and future anticipations (Trasmundi & Cowley, 2020). The embodied dimension of reading emphasises how sensory engagement (sight, scent, sound, and touch) combines with a reader's lived experience to create a dynamic, layered understanding of the text. This complexity arises from integrating historical and cultural contexts with the sensory and cognitive processes involved. The reader's body, shaped by accumulated encounters with texts, brings an embodied responsiveness that extends beyond the present moment, incorporating layers of lived experience (Di Paolo et al., 2018). Reading therefore, is not a solitary practice, but a multiscalar process that spans individual sensory engagement, socially learned habits, and broader socio-cultural structures. Over time, readers develop habits that scaffold their engagement with texts, forming a repertoire of nested embodied knowledge essential for sustaining reading as a practice. These include fundamental motor and perceptual skills – how to hold a book, the mechanics of page-turning, the appropriate reading direction, bodily positioning – as well as linguistic-symbolic skills such as recognising style, genre, and plot structures (Trasmundi, 2025). These skills, acquired through repeated interactions, contribute to what can be understood as 'social reading', a dynamic process shaped by guided attention to social affordances (Gibson, 1979; Jensen & Pedersen, 2016; Trasmundi, 2025). The more extensive a reader's historical engagement with texts and the deeper their expertise, the greater the landscape of affordances can be. Reading, then, is an active, embodied integration of habitual knowledge, and the ever-evolving terrain of textual meaning.

Pacemaking reflects the need for movement to sustain perception and understanding. Movement is linked with attention to create a temporal rhythm that enables cognitive engagement. Readers use this rhythm to modulate their pace, adjust their focus, and navigate the text. Pacemaking thus reflects how bodily dynamics sustain a particular flow of textual engagement. Shifts in pace is a break in a pattern of engagement. Pacemaking thus echoes the principles of wayfinding, where recalibrations in movement and orientation occur in response to environmental affordances (Heft, 1996). Just as a navigator pauses to reorient based on shifting cues, a reader's break functions as a moment of recalibration prompted by frustration, surprise, excitement, and insight – allowing for a renewed engagement with the text.

Readers (un)consciously respond to the rhythms embedded in the text by slowing down, pausing, or accelerating their reading. These shifts can be seen as breaks in the reading flow, creating moments for reflection, frustration, or imaginative engagement. The breaks can be welcomed or shot down depending on the reader's training, task, and awareness. By allowing these breaks readers open spaces for elaborate interactions with the text, where associations, new meanings, and connections emerge. Pacemaking incorporates a kinaesthetic dimension that is essential to understanding how readers inhabit and navigate a text beyond mere linguistic analysis. By studying how these rhythms unfold, we can gain insight into the embodied nature of reading and how different paces invite varying modes of cognitive and imaginative engagement and understanding.

Material engagement is a dimension inspired by the cognitive archaeologist, Lambros Malafouris' (2013) Material Engagement Theory (henceforth, MET). MET offers a framework for understanding how cognitive processes are shaped by material interactions. MET challenges the notion that cognition is solely internal, positing instead that the materials we interact with – whether tools or texts – play an active role in shaping our thinking. In reading, the materiality of the text – the form, medium, and physical properties – affects the reading experience, as it is not simply a cognitive task but a tactile, embodied one. Whether reading from a book or a screen, the material properties of the medium shape how we engage with the text.

At the heart of MET is the concept of 'material agency'. In reading, it means that text itself is not a conduit for meaning but a constituent in the cognitive process. This insight is crucial in contemporary reading practices where digital formats have transformed how we engage with texts (Wolf, 2018). The transition from printed to digital formats alters the tactile interaction with the text, and with it, the cognitive strategies readers employ. Words and symbols, whether on paper or screen, possess material properties that shape how we understand and navigate them. Malafouris critiques the fallacy of conflating semiotic ontologies by equating material signs with linguistic signs. He illustrates this with a quote from Bateson: 'The lions in Trafalgar Square could have been eagles or bulldogs and still have carried the same (or similar) messages about empire and about cultural premises of nineteenth-century England. And yet, how different might their message have been had they been made of wood!' (Bateson, 1973:130, in Malafouris, 2013:90–91). Despite the linguistic connotations of 'signs carrying meaning', the emphasis here is that materiality is an integral part of cognitive-affective processes, not just a transparent medium to uncover underlying meaning. Malafouris argues that the confusion lies in assuming that the linguistic sign 'vase' shares the same semiotic properties as the 'real ceramic vase'. I extend this argument by asserting that all signs – including words – possess material properties. Thus, the word 'vase', whether in linguistic form or as a physical object, has static-dynamic properties related to its material manifestation. Consequently, the medium through which text is read, be it printed or digital, impacts the reading experience, a topic I will explore empirically in Section 3.

Another key idea in MET is that of 'enactive signification', where meaning is not pre-given but emerges through the dynamic interactions between humans and their material environment. This process is exemplified in activities such as tool use, where the affordances of the tool and the intentions of the user co-create new possibilities for action. For instance, Malafouris provides empirical examples of how a potter's wheel is not just a passive instrument; its design and material properties influence the potter's movements and decisions, leading to a continuous feedback loop between the potter, the clay, and the wheel. MET can thus emphasise the physical act of reading – how we hold a book, move our eyes, and position our bodies – as it plays a crucial role in how we engage with the text.

MET also explores the temporal dimension of material engagement. It recognises that cognitive processes unfold over time and are influenced by the history of interactions between humans and materials. This temporal aspect is crucial for understanding how habits, skills, and cultural practices develop and evolve. For example, the repetitive use of a particular tool can lead to the development of specific motor skills and cognitive strategies unique to that tool's affordances. This insight is crucial in the current era of digitalisation, where reading materials are increasingly provided on digital devices rather than in printed versions. MET provides a robust framework for understanding cognition as a distributed, dynamic, and materially grounded phenomenon. By highlighting the active role of materials in shaping human thought and action, MET offers an ecological view of cognition that bridges the gap between mind and matter. It emphasises creation, that is the process of material engagement, such as a potter's engagement with plain clay, a musician's undecided engagement with an instrument, or a painter's engagement with the raw canvas. These artistic practices are inherently open-ended allowing for an expensive range of creative possibilities. In contrast, reading is constrained by the symbolic nature of text. While a potter can craft vases, a musician can compose new melodies, and a painter can create entirely new images, a reader's engagement is constrained not only by the medium (the book, or other textual form) but also by the written voice of the author. However, there is a sweet spot in reading where MET and the concept of breaks converge. In breaks, reading becomes more than linguistic interpretation of a fixed symbolic product; it transforms into an interactive, emergent process. Here, the Japanese concept of ma – the interval or space between elements – becomes crucial. The reader can navigate these gaps, dwelling on particular words, emphasising certain sounds, or engaging rhythms in ways that are uniquely shaped by her own embodied experience. Rather than being wholly determined by the author's intent, the reading process itself becomes a site of material engagement, where meaning is co-constructed through the interplay of text, cognition, and embodied interaction.

2.3.1 The Problem of Higher Cognitive Processes

The 4E cognition framework, which has shaped this imaginative approach to reading, have been extensively explored in team - and task-based and movement practices, such as material crafts, performance arts, and sports. However, they have received limited attention in the context of higher-order cognitive, solitary practices, such as reading, where the cognitive process unfolds in private, introspective ways. Yet rather than assuming that imagining requires internal stand-ins for absent entities, I emphasise the observable, embodied dynamics of reading, which reveal how imaginative engagement actually unfolds in real time. This involves contextualising reading behaviours within the broader ecology of textual structures, cultural backgrounds, and material engagements. By examining patterns across different reading settings, we can better understand how imagination is shaped not by static internal models but by interactions with external representational structures – texts, marks on a page, images, and even gestures. This dynamic modulation of attention and imagination is central to meaning-making but has often been overlooked in representation-heavy cognitive models (Kieverstein & Rietveld, 2018). The key challenge, then, is not to explain how the mind stores and retrieves representations but how readers dynamically perceive meaning through embodied and interactive engagement with texts and the wider environment.

It can be difficult to explain how readers engage with counterfactual ideas that do not have a direct environmental correlate. The challenge is to understand how readers navigate and make sense of such content purely through ecological and enactive means. Further, imaginative reading involves navigating through different temporal scales – recollecting past experiences, anticipating future possibilities, and engaging with the present moment in the text. This temporal modulation is complex and requires a nuanced understanding of how attention and imagination are coordinated over time. Traditional cognitive models often overlook these dynamics, focusing instead on local processes of comprehension.

While the theory of imaginative reading outlines a neat explanatory framework for the processes and properties that construct the practice, it needs an empirical, descriptive companion that can test these theoretical assumptions. For instance, an empirical description of the moments of ma can indicate cognitive engagement and the potential for significant imaginative exploration. Shifts in gaze reflect transitions in attention and the movement between different layers of the text or connections to personal experiences. Physical gestures, such as tracing words, underlining phrases, or mimicking actions described in the text, provide a tangible link to the imaginative process. An ecological cognitive ethnography provides such a framework, allowing us to study readers in real time and over time, and to make data comparative across different contexts. This approach helps us avoid the fallacy of representation by focusing on the actual, situated practices of readers, rather than abstracting their experiences into decontextualised cognitive models.

The following section introduces a cognitive ethnography of reading, presenting empirical examples of break patterns in natural reading settings. The idea of empirically exploring self-initiated breaks in reading is novel in reading research. This empirical investigation will further illustrate how readers navigate and benefit from dynamic, responsive reading trajectories, ultimately enriching our understanding of the imaginative power of reading.

3 A Cognitive Ethnography of Breaks in Imaginative Reading

> Social theory is largely a game of make-believe in which we pretend, just for the sake of argument, that there's just one thing going on: essentially, we reduce everything to a cartoon so as to be able to detect patterns that would be otherwise invincible. As a result, all real progress in social science has been rooted in the courage to say things that are, in the final analysis, slightly ridiculous: the work of Karl Marx, Sigmund Freud or Claude-Lévi Strauss being only particularly salient cases in point. One must simplify the world to discover something new about it. The problem comes when, long after the discovery has been made, people continue to simplify.
>
> **- Graeber and Wengrow, 2021:21**

3.1 Imaginative Reading in Real-Life Settings

In the previous sections, we explored the theoretical underpinnings of imaginative reading, emphasising the importance of multiscalar attention, pacemaking, and material engagement. These dimensions were developed based on Gibson's ecological approach to visual perception, Japanese dramaturgy, and Malafouris' material engagement theory to frame our understanding of these phenomena. Notably, no previous research has explored the importance of self-initiated microbreaks during reading, and therefore, there is an urgent need to fill that gap. Importantly, as Graeber and Wengrow caution, focusing on one thing – breaks – risks overstating their significance. It is thus important to clarify that this particular focus is not to suggest that breaks are the only meaningful moments in imaginative reading. Other moments, equally rich in imagination and crucial for reflection and creative thinking, undoubtedly exist. However, breaks deserve more attention, as they have been largely overlooked and undervalued in the dominant view of reading. Likewise, one can argue that rich imaginative reading is cognitively demanding and should thus not be the focus of all reading practices. I elaborate on this in the final Section 4, discussing when, where and how educators and readers might adopt a break-probing reading strategy. This section, however, systematically explores breaks, presenting them as fertile ground for imaginative engagement, waiting to be recognised within the broader context of reading research. Building on my own ethnographic studies, I suggest that these breaks are not passive interruptions but moments of heightened cognitive complexity. By analysing readers in real-world, non-experimental settings, we can observe how they shift their attention, pause to recalibrate, or engage embodied gestures that reflect ongoing cognitive and perceptual processes.

The goal of this section is not to provide an exhaustive empirical dataset on imaginative reading. Instead, it offers examples of specific readings that can: (i) inform the hypothesis that breaks are crucial for the reader's imaginative processes; and (ii) identify basic dimensions of imaginative reading relevant across contexts. I do not foreground the specific content or output of imaginative thinking. Instead, I explore how imagination in its broadest sense relates to the ability to manage pace, exploit, and endure the resulting tensions from engaging with those breaks. These processes are valuable not only to the particular content and outcome of reading but also because their emergence enables general experience with critical and reflective thinking that shape embodied habits of attention, and a particular sensitivity towards one's own pacemaking valuable for well-being more broadly (Mangen, 2008). While I can occasionally comment on the specific aspects of imagining content, it is often challenging because silent reading limits access to private understanding at a linguistic level. However, cognitive ethnography can interpret the overall function or significance in terms of embodied engagement during breaks. A natural next step in this research would be to explore the global function of imaginative processes – examining their quality in relation to reading tasks, their connection to reading experience and pleasure and their broader cognitive functions.

3.2 Cognitive Ethnography and Its Relevance for Imagination

Cognitive ethnography, coined by the cognitive anthropologist, Edwin Hutchins, in 1995, offers a unique lens for studying cognition by examining task-worlds in their natural settings. Hutchins's approach was a direct result of a critique directed towards cognitive anthropology, his own scholarly field[2]:

> Many of the foundational problems of cognitive science are consequences of our ignorance of the nature of cognition in the wild... The first part of the job is, therefore, a descriptive enterprise. I call this description of the cognitive task world a "cognitive ethnography." One might have assumed that cognitive anthropology would have made this sort of work its centerpiece. It has not. Studying cognition in the wild is difficult, and the outcomes are uncertain. (Hutchins, 1995:370ff)

Departing from traditional views that focus solely on brain-centred cognition, Hutchins's approach emphasises the distributed and ecosystemic nature of cognition. It redirects attention to the interactions among individuals and their environments, treating cognitive systems as distributed rather than isolated in individuals (Hutchins, 1995). As the methodology emphasises the importance of studying cognition as it unfolds in real-world settings, it positions itself as an 'outdoor' psychology in direct opposition to experimental cognitive science's focus on 'indoor' psychology (cf. Hutchins, 1995).

More recently, this approach has evolved towards more anti-representationalist and ecological perspectives, exploring not only functional coordination among components in a system but also imaginative and open-ended forms of living (Ormerod & Ball, 2000; Steffensen, 2013; Trasmundi, 2020, 2024; Trasmundi et al., 2024). As such, an ecological cognitive ethnography contextualises observations within broader frameworks while highlighting the diversity of human engagement in current activities (Trasmundi, 2020). It examines how individuals modulate their activities within their environments, considering factors beyond individual capabilities. One of the strengths of ecological cognitive ethnography is its ability to combine various observational techniques, facilitating learning from direct interactions and video recordings. This approach is particularly well-suited to understand dynamic embodiments in reading, which are difficult to measure in controlled laboratory settings. Unlike experimental paradigms that isolate reading as a discrete cognitive process, ethnographic observations reveal how readers actively shape their own reading trajectories through embodied pauses, gaze shifts, and interactive engagement with material texts and their overall reading context.

---

[2] For an elaborate introduction see Trasmundi (2020) and Ball & Ormerod (2000).

Moreover, cognitive ethnographers engage in dialogue with participants, probe into possibilities and alternative ways of thinking, enriching our understanding of human cognition and social practices. Questions like 'How can this be?' and 'Is there a different way?' extend beyond the immediate context and can be situated within a broader historical framework (cf. Trasmundi, 2024). Cognitive ethnography examines human coordination across multiple timescales, focusing on inter-bodily dynamics spanning behavioural, physiological, experiential, interpersonal, and cultural processes. This detailed examination of engagement is contextualised within the larger world, guarding against the oversimplifications that social theories can produce.

Combining social anthropology with cognitive ethnography grounds general narratives and global observations in empirical, local, and particular experiences. This approach ensures that particularities are considered within the broader contexts in which they operate. Anthropology's broad perspective enables the exploration of societies and cultures across diverse contexts and time periods, fostering the emergence of coherent, grand narratives. For instance, Tim Ingold has convincingly demonstrated how anthropological analysis can highlight significant shifts in our understanding of reading, critiquing the narrowness of the prevalent cognitivist perspective (Ingold, 2024). He contrasts modern reading practices with historical readings, such as medieval monks reading liturgical texts by tracing lines with their fingers and vocalising the words. This bodily approach to reading, he suggests, is much like inhabiting a landscape – a direct contrast to the detached, surface-level engagement of contemporary readers. He also uses an anthropology of reading to point out that changes in reading ecologies, like the shift from physical books to digital screens, alter our reading experiences and practices to the extent that we cannot think of them as similar activities (Ingold, 2024). These changes reflect technological innovations and societal priorities, and they have significant implications for education, where digital devices increasingly replace traditional print materials. Ingold's anthropology is inherently social, highlighting community practices, and depicting reading as a way of life for different groups, such as medieval monks or modern screen readers. However, its social interest downplays ontogenetic processes or the interplay between social and personal aspects of life. This is where cognitive ethnography excels, revealing the nuanced ways individuals navigate these tensions within social practices. It compares not only screen readers to print readers but also explores differences within these categories, uncovering the multifaceted nature of cultural practices. That is, cognitive ethnography reveals the nuanced trajectories of distinct yet interconnected events, showing how different features and tensions coexist within a social practice and shape its development. This synergy adds depth and vibrancy to the understanding of human forms of life, here in the case of reading.

In summary, conceptual work must be traced to experience, and experience should be categorised within a broader social conceptual framework. The theory of imaginative reading presented in this Element emerged from theoretical discussions and empirical observations. Particularly, it emerged from empirical observations of how breaks emerge as readers engage in ways that cannot be explained by reference to representational operations. That is, the theory of imaginative reading is continuously emerging from and tested against ethnographic empirical work to illustrate its validity. The following ethnography of reading[3] thus presents small excerpts that inform the theory of imaginative reading. This section is divided pragmatically into three parts, each illustrating how breaks are important for one of the three dimensions – multiscalarity, pacemaking, and material engagement – that constitute the theoretical framework. As discussed in Section 2, these dimensions are intertwined and cannot be understood in isolation. However, they are presented sequentially here for the sake of clarity and argument.

3.3 Breaks in Imaginative Reading

3.3.1 Multiscalarity in Reading

Imagining Life in a Giant Pear

To illustrate the concept of multiscalarity in reading, I present a case involving a ten-year-old boy reading to his younger brother with their mother also present. He reads aloud from Jakob Martin Strid's fairytale: *The Incredible Story about the Giant Pear*,[4] a book featuring colourful illustrations and handwritten text. The story revolves around a giant pear, carved out and used as a boat by fantastical characters solving various mysteries.

Overall, the boy demonstrated excellent reading skills, but if viewed through a code-based lens, his performance might appear impaired or unfocused in certain points. At some point, for instance, he suddenly starts to hesitate,

---

[3] All the following examples are drawn from my video-ethnographic studies on reading. Some of this data has been published previously, though not with a focus on breaks; thus, where relevant, I reference these sources. Before introducing each example, I provide its ethnographic context to ensure the necessary background for understanding the argument. All ethical and legal approvals, including informed consent, have been strictly adhered to throughout the research. While each study was shaped by its own epistemological concerns, I draw on data from all previous studies to explore the diversity of breaks in reading across cultures, genres, ages, and tasks. As a result, the dataset spans multiple longitudinal reading studies (up to three years), supported by the Danish Research Council (grant numbers: 1130-00008A & 8108-00005B). Overall, the dataset encompasses a broad spectrum of reading settings and participants across varied ages, expertise levels, and cultural backgrounds. It includes a range of genres and reading materials, from screens to printed texts, used for both leisure and academic purposes. The study examines children's reading —both individual and joint sessions—as well as university-level adult readers.

[4] Danish original title: *Den utrolige historie om den kæmpestore pære*

Figure 2 A young reader's gaze shift during reading. The boy pauses, looks away from the text, and appears to imagine living in the story world, showing how reading fosters immersive, affective engagement.

gazes across the pages, and occasionally stops reading aloud. However, when putting these breaks and behaviours into a broader context, his pauses, guesses, misspellings, and gaze-wandering, indicate his engagement in imaginative work. As an example, at one point, the boy looked at the drawing of the pear (see Figure 2, picture A) and exclaimed excitedly, 'OH I would like to try and live there, man – there is a massive amount of food!'[5]

The boy is not just decoding symbols; he is actively engaging with possible worlds, imagining life in a giant pear and the affective associations that follow (see also Trasmundi & Cowley, 2020) for an extensive analysis of this boy's reading). His outburst indicates his projection into the story, imagining what it must be like to live in a giant pear. Such moments of imaginative engagement are crucial for the joy of reading, sparking creative skills by linking the text with personal preferences and desires. However, in functional cognitive terms, this imaginative work comes at the expense of fluency, speed, and accuracy. Further, he glanced at his mother for two seconds before resuming his reading (see Figure 2, picture B). Seeking a response, he was instead guided by her gaze to continue reading in the narrow sense of the word. The boy's rapid return to scanning the text reflects a self-correction to align with expected reading behaviour, suppressing his spontaneous imaginative engagement. His behaviour suggests that educational norms highlighted by the mother's gaze and ignorance favours fluency and accuracy over exploratory breaks in ways that might

---

[5] Danish original: ÅRH jeg vil gerne prøve at bo der, mand – der er ordentlig meget mad!

inadvertently discourage the young reader from developing flexible, break-probing reading strategies. In the observations, it was evident how his joy decreased, and as his smile vanished, his voice became less cheerful as he continued his task of reading aloud. Although this case focuses on early reading development, its relevance extends beyond childhood. The ways in which readers are trained to prioritise fluency and minimise hesitation can have long-term effects on how they engage with texts later in life. If break-probing engagement is discouraged from an early stage, adult readers may be less likely to employ reflective, self-paced strategies in silent reading, defaulting instead to a habit of uninterrupted, efficiency-driven reading. This suggests that reading norms shaped in early literacy practices may continue to influence how readers navigate and regulate their engagement with texts well into adulthood (Trasmundi, 2025).

Observing the emotional rollercoaster of the boy – from dutiful reading to utmost excitement and back to dutiful reading again – was almost painful. This observation prompted me to revisit the literature on breaks in reading and imagination research, revealing a crucial dimension in reading research that has not been adequately addressed. The ethnographic data also prompted questions such as: Why did the boy not exploit this imaginative process further? Why did the mother not show interest but instead guided his attention back to scanning? And why do these moments seem impossible to recapture after the reading, as their motivation apparently lies in the actual process of experiencing?

A few days later, the boy reads aloud to his mother from a schoolbook. At one moment he encounters a new word 'weaving' in the phrase articulated by a female character: 'I am weaving dream cloths, she said'.[6] The boy pauses and asks his mother, 'What is weaving?' The mother replies, 'It is a kind of craft, but the artifact is a bit like ... Well, I can show you afterward'. The boy's momentary curiosity is dismissed, and he returns to reading the text aloud, and the topic is never revisited. Once again, the ethnographic observations show how the joy of reading that arises in such expanded moments can be abruptly shut down and disregarded – unfortunately, in a way that diminishes the overall enjoyment of reading, especially if repeated over time.

Memory and Imagining: Making Names of Known Sounds

A few moments later, the same boy struggles with the genitive form of the word 'heart' (DA: hjerte) in the sentence 'the heart's red blood' (DA: hjertets røde blod). He repeats it several times but slightly incorrectly as he misses the final 't' and making it sound like 'hjertes' instead of the correct 'hjertets'. In fact, he enjoys this difficulty, and he laughs as he repeatedly attempts to make the

---

[6] Danish original: *Jeg væver drømmeklæder, sagde hun.*

correct pronunciation. In this situation, the mother encourages him to read it out loud correctly and supports his attempts and struggling. Next, in Figure 3, picture A, we observe his emotional pleasure in the reading, suggesting that the struggling is not a problem but actually sparks his interest in learning and probing.

He continues reading, and fails four times, repeatedly saying 'hjertes' instead of 'hjertets' (heart's). This repeated error leads to an unexpected insight, and he suddenly comments: 'It almost sounds like a name ... Heart's ... red blood'[7], implying that it refers to a person's (Heart's) red blood rather than the biological heart's red blood. In Danish, heart is *hjerte,* which is in fact a rare name (Hjerte). As he shares this insight, he gazes at his mother with a smile on his face (Figure 3, picture B.) Compared to the articulation problems, this sophisticated and creative insight goes unacknowledged by the mother. As she avoids responding to his comment, he resumes reading out load, and his emotional engagement decreases significantly, see Figure 3, picture C. The boy's curiosity goes unrewarded, as his implicit question – 'it almost sounds like a name' – receives neither confirmation nor rejection. Although he is correct, his intuition remains unacknowledged, and his mother's lack of interest subtly signals to him what is deemed important, and not, in reading. While it is possible that the observational setting influenced the mother's reaction, this moment nonetheless highlights how reading norms are socially reinforced. The mother's immediate correction reflects a broader tendency to prioritise fluency and accuracy as the

  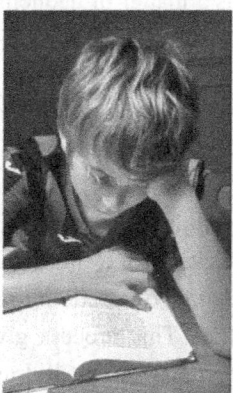

Figure 3 A child's reading journey from curiosity to disengagement. The boy offers an imaginative interpretation, receives no response from the adult, and resumes reading with reduced enthusiasm.

---

[7] Danish original: *Det lyder næsten som et navn ... Hjertes ... røde blod.*

primary goals of reading, subtly discouraging pauses, hesitations, or exploratory engagement *during* reading – despite no inherent reason why these elements could not be integrated. This interaction illustrates how cultural expectations around reading shape not only formal education but also everyday reading practices, influencing how children habituate ideas of what 'proper' reading should be like.

The boy's reading is multiscalar in the sense that he breaks the local, continuous scanning of words, and uses this rupture to connect various scales. He uses his engagement with the text to play with ideas about names and to learn about novel words and sounds, but his ludic parenthesis in his continuous scanning is not rewarded. As his attempt to explore this, in this case with his mother, it not successful, he adapts to the socio-cultural norm of reading which guides his attention to continuous engagement. However, his immediate and almost impulsive temporal integrational behaviour reflects insights about reading dynamics from eye-tracking experiments: 'The speed of the eye's motion across the page – but not the motion itself – interferes with perception, and it is only during the brief pause between movements that we actually "read"' (Manguel, 2014:37). This evidence supports my point that all reading is imaginative. However, if readers are allowed and trained to extend breaks further, they can more deliberately link timescales in ways that allow ideas and impressions to percolate, sediment, and become manifest anchors for intelligent and significant reflection.

So, why do we not train this systematically, this divergent form of reading? This, I suggest, is because we experience, teach and model reading as linear and as a matter of deducing fixed meaning. This understanding has shaped educational systems in a way that over time guide readers' attention away from deliberate breaks and towards an efficient and economic scanning strategy. Some of those questions are addressed in the literature. For instance, it has been argued that the pursuit of perfection is important for student readers (Jensen, 2023), which means maintaining attention on the ocular scanning and not disengaging from the attentional standards. Further, rich imaginative flickers, like the ones observed earlier, can only occur when there is some degree of freedom to reconstruct previous experiences with real-time perception. This process gives reading an imaginative, multiscalar, and dialogical component, but it draws on temporal processes that conflict with the scale of fluent, stable engagement. Unfortunately, educational practices often train the opposite, deeming such moments as task-switching, lack of concentration, and irrelevant distractions (Trasmundi et al., 2024; Wig et al., 2025).

3.3.2 Pacemaking in Reading: Rhythms and Tensions Shape Ideas and Attention

Exploiting Space-Time

One remarkable observation from the ethnographic reading data, was how several readers demonstrated a change in their engagement, characterised by an observable whole-bodied attempt to endure complexity in thinking. The scene I describe here is marked by emerging hesitation, much like the Noh performers on stage describe the moment building up to the ma and senu hima. Likewise, Ingold describes imagining as a process always present, sometimes lurking in the background, sometimes taking the front seat. He argues that there is:

> a kind of imagination that is always shooting of in the distance; and a material engagement that is always holding us back. And this is a particular tension that humans experience. Any artist will agree on that ... Imagine you are a composer, and the music is shooting ahead in your imagination, and you are struggling with this pen and paper trying to notate it down on manuscript paper. And a really hard work of composition is holding it there – the imagination – so you can get it down. And there is a constant anxiety that it will all going to slip away from you before you manage to catch it. And I think that is really the root of human life – the imagination. (Ingold, 2021)

This idea aligns with the case examples below, illustrating how readers manage multiple complex processes by employing embodied strategies to contain tension. The Figure 4 exemplifies these moments across different reading contexts, genres, languages, purposes, and text lengths.[8] What unites them is the observable affective tension as readers strive to hold everything together. This challenge is evident in their facial and gestural expressions. For instance, they extend their gestural expressions in space for several seconds before transitioning into another rhythmic pattern. Sometimes this leads to exclamations of insight, joy, or frustration. However, each phase reveals a pattern of heightened attention and slow textual engagement. One strategy, as illustrated in Figure 4, pictures A–C, involves holding on to certain elements (using fingers as placeholders for thought or text) while simultaneously exploring other spaces, either within or beyond the text.

In Figure 4, picture A, the female reader preserves an impression by marking its significance with an outstretched arm, all while searching for elements in the text. Similarly, in Figure 4, picture B, the male reader uses his index finger to mark something as significant, while his upward gaze suggests, paraphrasing

---

[8] The readers presented in Figure 4 come from two different studies. The readers in Pictures A and B are Danish BA students engaged in study reading for different courses. They are affiliated with a Danish University. The reader in Picture C is a master's student from another Danish university, also engaged in study reading.

Figure 4 Strategic anchoring in reading: readers use hands and gaze to manage attention and hold cognitive and textual positions during reflective engagement.

Ingold, that he is doing *really hard work of composition, holding it there – the imagination – so he can get it down*. This interplay between material and immaterial activity is carefully managed, allowing him to maintain his place in the physical text (holding onto the book and his position) while simultaneously deepening his thoughts. In Figure 4, picture C, the female reader integrates multiple texts, shifting her gaze between them and using her fingers to track her position, allowing her to alternate seamlessly between texts and maintain focus without losing momentum.

In other studies, such as dance choreography (Ravn, 2017) or poetry recitation (Gibbs, 2017), sensory-motor contingencies have shown to have a stronger impact on memory than mental processing (Noë, 2004). By hypothesis, a reader can exploit multiple bodily resources at the same time to manage complexity and thus contain tension: she can point, mimic, vocalise, move, and so on. which supports the integration of cognitive-embodied processes. When the narrative unfolding suddenly is interrupted from its predicted trajectory, all kinds of scenarios can play out: the past, present, and future are in tension. Yet ma, in reading has a cost; it requires extreme attention control, and thus only emerges at significant places. In Noh this is described as an enigma: 'Paradoxically, it necessarily requires more effort for the Noh actor to retain this posture of not-doing, and activate the internal sensitivity of his mind' (Morioka, 2015:90). Likewise, in reading, managing tensions in breaks and shifts might be exhaustive, hence there is a need to empirically test when, how, and to which extend such breaks fuel valuable processes, and also what the downside might be.

Pacemaking refers to the reader's temporal progression in reading, which is not a stable, smooth, or continuous trajectory but rather a punctuated, dynamic path. The key idea is that the more a reader engages in a break-based, varied reading pattern, the more their imaginative power will manifest experientially, enhancing creative and critical engagement. I have demonstrated that shifts in pace are crucial, particularly in moments where cognitive and experiential processes converge at a brink point, creating a paradoxical feeling of being on the verge of both breakthrough and breakdown. This can be observed in the boy's gesturing (Figure 4, picture B) and the girl's furrowed eyebrows (Figure 4, picture A), indicating an intense effort to maintain focus and not let the moment slip away, in Ingold's terms. Such moments are rewarding and cognitively and affectively rich, but also demanding, as the readers claim in the succeeding interviews. The students explain that these moments are experienced as both important and exhausting. This ambiguity reflects Dewey's idea, that such moments are painful and intriguing at the same time. Further, those processes train concentration and creative processes in a particularly sense-dense manner. The pace changes as attention shifts from engaging with textual marks to a gestural reorganisation that either puts ocular scanning on hold or slows it down significantly. As observed in the gallery, these moments of merging and maximal temporal integration offer alternatives to the traditional reading process, which we will explore further.

Creating Temporal Loopholes

While all readers across the dataset exhibited breaks, they varied significantly in their distribution – including duration, emotional expression, and strategies for either leveraging or suppressing these moments. Some readers actively used breaks to deepen engagement, while others minimised or tried to avoid them to maintain fluency, reflecting individual differences in reading habits, experience, and contextual demands. Some readers create loopholes, moments of ma, allowing them to engage open-endedly with elaborate ideas in a more sequential or accumulative manner without losing track of the overall agenda. This pattern is primarily observed through shifts in gaze. The pace changes from fluent ocular scanning to a fixation on a distant point (often up in the air or straightforward), transforming the dynamic pace into one that is rather motionless. Alternatively, the readers shift their gaze from the page and also initiate a gestural rhythm, such as tapping, nodding, or mumbling. I will provide a few empirical examples of this pattern coming from both interview data and video-observation of reading practices across Danish and Japanese reading practices.

Figure 5, picture A is from an interview with a Japanese university student who describes how he experiences ma in reading. He argues that, in reading, he often needs a moment . . . to read. He elaborates this in relation to ma which he especially experiences as: 'spaces between chapters or sections that create moments to breathe and pause. On paper, it happens when I turn the pages.

Figure 5 Self-initiated pauses: readers create reflective space (ma) by looking away or flipping pages, integrating moments of embodied interpretation.

Ma is important to understand what the book says. In digital texts, it just flashes away, but page-turning creates moments to process. I like to read and turn pages back and forth to understand'. He illustrates how he creates ma himself when puzzled and the text does not invite a break; he initiates a back-and-forth flipping strategy, turning a page from side to side to insert a moment of reflection as many times as needed before he resumes scanning. Ingold (2022:191) likewise emphasises the importance of page-turning: 'To turn a page is like the wayfarer's turning a corner, or surmounting a pass, at which point a new vista opens up ahead'. The turn itself becomes the moment where anticipation and the unknown converge. It seems crucial for both imagining and the joy in reading. This understanding also points to the fact that people find reading without page-turning exhausting (e.g. screen reading), and why many children find pleasure in managing the page-turning even when their parents read to them.

The most usual break was observed as gazing up and fixating the gaze in the air. This strategy is observed across cultural reading practices as illustrated in Figure 5, pictures B and C. Readers would repeatedly elicit and engage in such moments, lasting from milliseconds to seconds, and occasionally even minutes. Across the large, cross-cultural dataset, it is observed how this form of pace-making invites a more open-ended and exploratory, affective process, similar to mind-wandering, creative, critical idea generation, and reflection. The reader's thoughts during these moments are less important than the pattern of engagement, which reveals a significant cognitive-affective form of focused involvement. However, further empirical testing is needed to explore how break patterns are distributed in relation to skill, genre, medium, motivation, culture, language, personality, task, and so on. Notably, in the current dataset, breaks showed significant variation in their patterns and frequencies across different participants. Some readers found breaks frustrating, feeling that interruptions hindered their reading flow and cognitive processes. As a result, they immediately shut those moments down, and did not extend them or exploit them further. In contrast, other readers (as those in Figure 5) enjoyed allowing their minds to wander and explore their thoughts before returning to textual reading.

3.3.3 Material Engagement

Haptic Reading

All reading, as previously mentioned, is multi-sensory. Of particular importance, and at the same time somewhat neglected in theories of reading, is the extent to which reading is an activity involving and requiring manual dexterity – that is, skilful handling by our fingers and hands. Rather than disappearing into the heated debate about the distinctive differences between the materiality of print books and digital texts, I draw on the core argument that all reading involves tactile experiences and thus shaped by the physical engagement with the text (Mangen, 2008).

Recognising the tactile and haptic nature of reading expands our understanding of how engagement with a text is inherently material. This perspective highlights how the physical act of reading – through manual dexterity and bodily movements – contributes not only to cognitive processes but also to the experiential dimensions of the activity. The focus here is on the diverse strategies of material engagement with texts, showing that the material is not simply a medium but an integral constituent of cognition itself. The materiality of reading shapes the task in ways that can both enhance and limit the experience.

Next, I will demonstrate a cross-section of the various strategies of material engagement in reading (which is not at all exhaustive). I will briefly demonstrate such forms of engaging and then reflect on their potential value for imaginative reading. The first example relates to fidgeting and attention control.

Fidgeting Regulates Attention and Reduces Tensions and Stress

Fidgeting during reading often involves touching and folding the pages. This fidgeting is not aligned with anticipated page-turning or other task-oriented actions. The data reveals that children, in particular, use their hands in this manner to manage attention and release tension during reading – likely because of their relative limited level of expertise and because reading aloud, the default mode for young children, induces more stress than silent reading (Kristensen et al., 2024). When they struggle with processes like articulation, sound reconstruction, or word recognition, they often fidget with the pages, engaging in dynamic, rhythmic bodily movements.

The boy uses different fidgeting strategies as he struggles with articulation. In Figure 6, pictures A–C, he both strokes and rolls the pages as he reads. His

  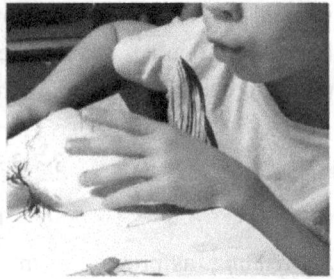

Figure 6 Fidgeting during reading: physical gestures emerge during cognitive strain, serving as attention regulation and rhythmic engagement tools.

fidgeting increases precisely at moments where he encounters higher cognitive demands or experience mild frustration. Also, his exaggerated mouth expression, indicates that he is using cognitive effort on achieving precision in the coordination between text, gaze, sound, and mouth movement (Figure 6, picture C). This description aligns with research indicating that fidgeting serves as a regulatory mechanism for attention and stress management (Farley et al., 2013). The rhythmic bodily engagement seen in these images suggests that micro-changes, such as tactile interactions with the book, can help sustain focus by preventing cognitive overload, rather than indicating distraction or disengagement. This observation is intriguing because the fidgeting occurs when hesitation emerges – when utterances slow down, mimicking becomes more salient (see Figure 6, picture C), and bodily movement patterns change significantly, imbuing a form of rhythmic engagement. Farley et al. (2013:2) suggest that: 'Fidgeting may represent an overt action that interacts with systems supporting the ability to sustain attention and thus act as a potential route to optimise attention. One possibility is that fidgeting might provide a form of a "mental break". This break is a ma moment where bodily pacemaking changes and allows task performance to continue instead of breaking down. The pacemaking inhibits fixation because hands and body engage in ways that necessitate a moving-on attitude. This insight aligns with psychological research emphasising how fidgeting is 'known to be related to stress in that individuals tend to fidget more while under stress (cf. Barash, 1974) and fidgeting appears to actually mediate the experience of perceived stress in some people (Mohiyeddini & Semple, 2013; Mohiyeddini et al., 2013)' (Farley et al., 2013). Furthermore, Farley and colleagues (2013) report on studies showing how fidgeting can help individuals sustain attention by increasing physiological changes and arousal. Research by Levine et al. (2000) demonstrates that energy expenditure increases significantly during non-exercise activities with sitting while fidgeting increasing energy expenditure by 54 per cent on average compared to sitting at rest. Even small fidgeting movements can have a pronounced effect. For instance, Andrade (2010) found that participants who doodled during a monotonous task improved their performance, which was attributed to an increase in overall arousal.

Such results highlight the potential value of focusing on the role of the hands and embodied interaction with reading materials in educational settings. Rather than viewing fidgeting as a distraction, educators could embrace it as a natural part of cognitive engagement. By allowing students to physically interact with books – handling, flipping pages, or even tracing words with their fingers – teachers can create a more dynamic, tactile reading experience also at an advanced level.

Imagining Hands

Another related aspect of tactile engagement with the material is related to the imagining processes that emerge from narrative engagement. In the gallery following, we revisit the boy from the first example, where he just has read about how the giant pear rolled down a hill and splashed into the sea. This narrative is explored further by the boy who uses the narrative, the visual aids in the book, and the large pages to gesture the pear's path in space.

Figure 7, pictures A and B correspond to the narrative description, indicating how the pear rolled down and into the sea: The boy uses his hands to trace a half-circle on the page, symbolising the pear's trajectory from the hill into the sea. In Figure 7, picture C he illustrates the splash, symbolised by his hand's flat pressure on the page. He then gestures how the pear bounces back to the surface of the sea and regains balance (Figure 7, picture D), making the narrative both representative of the text and something more, as he uses his hands to imagine in a way that adds aesthetic-embodied dimensions such as force, speed, and movement.

Figure 7 Embodied narrative engagement: the child uses his hands to simulate motion, force, and rhythm, transforming static illustrations into dynamic story enactments.

50   *Creativity and Imagination*

This experience is highly tactile, enhancing memory as it is experienced both through narrative style and the gymnastics of his hands. Such an imaginative process requires the boy to initiate a ma or break from textual scanning, engaging with the text in a way facilitated by the book's design – its size, font, colourful pictures, and thick, large pages. Likewise, Manguel (2014) underlines that the design of the book is not just an aesthetic and symbolic feature, but indeed functional and a result of usage and practices: 'I judge a book by its cover; I judge a book by its shape. ... From the beginning, readers demanded books in formats adapted to their intended use' (Manguel, 2014:125). The boy's interaction not only deepens his comprehension but also makes the reading experience more vivid and memorable. And crucially, it depends on reading beyond the lines, enacting ma as part of reading. This observation also indicates that materiality matters, and readers care about the quality of the books.

Manually Structuring Perception-Action

Another noteworthy observation concerns the use of hands and tools to maintain attention on the relevant part of the text and to narrow down the perceptual field. This technique ensures that the mind remains undisturbed by excessive complexity or prompts that invite further engagement. In print reading, this strategy is particularly effective, as the substrate can be manipulated in three-dimensional space. In the gallery (Figure 8), we observe how young children aged 5–7 read in Danish and English at their homes. It becomes clear how available tools and materials, as well as the hands are used to structure the reading.

In Figure 8 various tools and hands are depicted. The use of post its (Figure 8, picture A), fingers (Figure 8, picture B), paper (Figure 8, picture C), and even an old piece of packaging (Figure 8, picture D) function to hide and reveal portions of the text gradually. This approach allows readers to break the reading into smaller, nested chunks, enhancing focus and concentration. As the reader

Figure 8 Manual scaffolding in early reading: young readers use hands and materials to structure attention, create pauses, and manage cognitive load.

moves forward, their hands shift the materials or fingers to expose new sections of the text. Much like turning pages, these small movements, such as shifting a finger or piece of paper, introduce subtle pauses, or ma, in the reading flow. I further observed in these ethnographic data, that these pauses often align with the reader's breathing patterns and small gestural adjustments, such as repositioning fingers or moving the paper at natural intervals. In several instances, readers appeared to pause at key moments – such as before difficult passages, after encountering unfamiliar words, or when anticipating the resolution of a sentence – and these pauses were accompanied by slight bodily adjustments. The rhythmic synchronisation between breath, hand movement, and reading pace suggests that manual engagement structures reading as a temporal, embodied process rather than a purely abstract one.

This observation is significant because it highlights how print reading involves more than just visual information pick-up; it is interwoven with bodily rhythms (i.e. breathing, pointing etc.) that shape engagement and understanding. These subtle, self-paced rhythms, which allow for the recalibration of attention and imaginative projection, exemplify what I refer to as 'the imagination pulse'. It captures how reading unfolds in a dynamic interplay between sensory-motor engagement, cognitive anticipation, and affective resonance. Further, reading is managed through a myriad of different technologies, which relates directly to how imaginative reading is constrained: 'Forms of imagination are inseparable from the material characteristics of modes, from their shaping in a society's history, and from their consequent interaction with the sensoriness, the sensuousness, of our bodies' (Kress, 2003:171 in Mangen, 2008). In the data, a consistent pattern was identified: digital reading tends to maintain a more static and fixed distance between the reader's head and the text, resulting in less dynamic bodily engagement, whereas reading on print enabled more vibrant and break-probing embodiment. Here, I present a gallery of readers, both children and adults, engaging with various texts for different purposes. For this discussion, the key is to illustrate how texts on smartphones, computers, and in print constrain movement control and shape the reading experience in distinct ways.

In Figure 9, picture A, the act of page-turning is much more dynamic and tactilely salient than the scrolling observed in Figure 9, pictures B and C. When engaging with a book, the coordination between body and text allows for a diverse range of interactions. In contrast, computers being less mobile, offer a more constrained set of ergonomic options. Smartphones, due to their smaller screen size, limit the spatial field of information, requiring more precise control over reading flow, such as line tracking and screen scrolling. Naturally, the reader's experience is shaped by the specific engagement with the text and the

Figure 9 Reading mediums and bodily interaction: physical books afford varied ergonomic engagement, while digital platforms impose constrained gestures and attention flow.

medium. Observations from Figure 9, pictures D, E, and F, demonstrate that printed books generally afford a more dynamic and varied reading distance. Unlike digital screens, holding and manipulating a physical book involves more than just turning pages; it requires the reader to feel its weight, texture, and physical fragility. Notably, the reader in Figure 9, picture F, mentioned in a follow-up interview, that the size and weight of the book necessitated continuous physical adjustments, influencing muscle tension and bodily posture. During the observations, it became evident that he frequently shifted his sitting position and altered how he held the book to maintain comfort and avoid exhaustion. This suggests that print-based reading fosters a more adaptive, embodied interaction, where engagement is not only cognitive but also shaped by physical affordances and constraints of the medium. Mangen elaborates:

> The reading process and experience of a digital text are greatly affected by the fact that we click and scroll, in contrast to tactilely richer experience when flipping through the pages of a print book. When reading digital texts, our haptic interaction with the text is experienced as taking place at an indeterminate distance from the actual text, whereas when reading print text we are physically and phenomenologically (and literally) in touch with the material substrate of the text itself. This may seem a matter of marginal importance in reading research, but I will claim – and show in the following – that it is a matter requiring attention as much more than a mantra for media theorists, or topic of interest mainly to philosophers: materiality matters. (Mangen, 2008:405)

The readers, in my ethnographic studies, are all digital natives. Nevertheless, the majority reported a preference for reading printed texts. However, practical constraints often limit their access to print materials, as many required texts are either unavailable or prohibitively expensive (Baron & Mangen, 2021).

Spatio-Temporal Overview and Interactive Trace-Making

Mangen et al. (2019) have discussed the importance of reading hands for memory in reading. The weight of a book and its narrative structure are connected to the physical location on the page and within the book as a whole. They also show how readers interpret the narrative in relation to the length of the book, considering how much text is left and what might happen in the forthcoming pages. This intuitive sense of length shapes imaginative processes, influencing expectations about how much can unfold and the level of detail likely to be described. This information is less immediate in digital versions, where readers lose the tangible sense of the book as a physical, discrete object, and the progression through its pages. As Tim Ingold notes, the lost palimpsest effect in digital reading environments strips away the layered, tactile experience of engaging with a physical book.

The tangible interaction with a book enhances the reader's engagement and allows the reader to carve out places of potential relevance in the book. This will be elaborated through a few examples from readers we have previously encountered: a student from a Japanese university, readers from two Danish universities, and the boy who read to his mother from his schoolbook.

In Figure 10, picture A, the reader keeps her fingers on one page even after turning it, marking particular areas that are easy to return to if needed. This often leads to an intersection of turning back and forth as the reader engages in higher cognitive processes like reflection or critical thinking with what is read and what the reader thinks about it. In Figure 10, picture B, the reader puts her wrist on the book to keep it open on a certain page while grabbing another book, enabling co-reading and synthetic reading facilitated by the physical affordances of the texts. These forms of material engagements, as suggested by the data, allow for complex cognitive and imaginative processes. The hands function as placeholders, allowing ma to emerge without losing track of the progression in reading. It becomes easy to resume scanning as the hands serve as material anchors, marking exactly where the reader started to read beyond the lines. Furthermore, readers often leaf through the book to get a tactile and visual sense of their progress; this process is illustrated in Figure 10, picture C. Leafing through a book involves experiencing the thickness and texture of its pages, engaging the reader's tactile and spatial awareness. This sensitivity to the book

Figure 10 Hands as anchors in reflective reading: readers use touch, motion, and annotation to manage spatial orientation, track ideas, and deepen interpretation during non-linear reading. Across contexts (pictures A–G), we observe how bodily strategies such as marking, flipping, pausing, and annotating help externalise memory and support analytical engagement with the text. These embodied techniques reveal reading as an active and situated practice, shaped by material interaction as much as cognitive intention.

as a physical object also aids memory recall, allowing readers to associate words, events, and descriptions with specific locations[9] – both on the page and within the broader narrative structure; something that came up repeatedly in the follow-up interviews.

Finally, reading is rarely about simply making letter-sound correspondences. Instead, it often involves managing multiple nested activities within the broader practice of reading. These activities are practically limitless, but in the dataset, they

---

[9] Regarding measures related to chronology and temporality, readers who used print pocket books performed better than those who read on a Kindle. While overall comprehension was similar between the two media, the lack of kinaesthetic feedback with a Kindle made it more challenging for readers to efficiently locate events within the text and understand the story's temporality. We suggest that achieving a correct spatial representation of the text, and consequently a coherent temporal organization of the story, relies on the sensorimotor cues provided by physically manipulating the book (cf. Mangen et al., 2019).

include writing, pointing, talking, moving, and gesturing, often in overlap. In the cases stated previously, the readers use a mix or writing practices; they duplicate, elaborate, add notes, highlight, and mark aspects of the text which creates a personalised hierarchy of relevance. Writing serves as an externalisation of individual judgment, leaving behind material traces that can later shape and inform future readings. In Figure 10, picture G, the readers' annotations illustrate a diverse range of strategies, highlighting the variability in how they interact with and structure their engagement with the text. However, some readers revealed in the follow-up interviews that they did not have time for this type of engagement. Their focus was on 'staying on the page' and avoiding disruptions caused by uncontrolled ideas or questions. These interview insights suggest that some readers perceive even minor adjustments or breaks as a threat to their understanding of how reading is achieved.

Socio-Material Engagement

Reading is not always a solitary and private activity. Especially in the early years, it is highly social and dialogical. Think of examples of parents who read to their children, and children practising their reading at home or in school. This form of social reading is also where the richness of imagining with the text is easiest to depict for the observer. Below are a few examples of social reading in children's early reading practises within their homes, illustrating this point.

In Figure 11, picture A, the listener (in the left side of the picture) comments on the reading, anticipates what will happen next, and asks questions, often in the middle of a sentence, enhancing the imaginative potential of the text. The listener here, co-creates breaks or ma. Depending on the main reader, these interruptions can be welcomed as an intriguing part of the reading process or ignored if they disrupt the ambition of fluent reading. At this stage of becoming a reader, those ma moments occurred more frequently than around structured school contexts. This pattern suggests that breaks are more naturally integrated and accepted among young readers, and in non-institutional contexts. Co-reading among children is often messy, highly fragmented, imaginative, and dialogical. However, I observed that parents reading aloud to their children tended to become increasingly frustrated when interrupted by questions or spontaneous storytelling. Parents would correct these interruptions, often responding with phrases such as, 'We will have to wait and see' or 'Please let me read, and then we can hear what you have to say afterward'. However, in many cases, the 'afterward' never fully captured the excitement or insight the child had at the moment of its emergence.

In Figure 11, picture B, the listener (not visible in the picture) acts as the page-turner, actively deciding when to move on, which influences the flow and engagement with the text. This constant negotiation of the reading pace fosters disturbances and dialogue, also concerning and negotiating how to engage with the text. In Figure 11, picture C, we see how reading is co-organised, with both participants holding the material and collaboratively guiding their focus. This strengthens their shared understanding and mutual support. The adult's role is crucial in shaping how ma moments influence the developing reader's future reading habits. Through material engagement and reading aloud, the adult helps regulate the flow of reading within a social context, implicitly modelling how breaks and rhythms contribute to meaning-making.

Alberto Manguel, in his reflections on reading aloud to the nearly blind Jorge Luis Borges, captures the social impact of breaks in reading: 'I would discover a text by reading it aloud, while Borges used his ears, as others use their eyes, to scan the page. When I read he'd interrupt, commenting on the text in order (I think) to take note of it in his mind' (Manguel, 2014:17). Through his ongoing commentary, Borges forced Manguel to break his usual style of attending, making him aware of how much he learned to read beyond the lines 'through a vastly entangled method of learned significances, social conventions, previous readings, personal experiences and private taste' (Manguel, 2014:37). Manguel relates his own experience to the Argentinian writer Martinez Estrada, who described this form of reading as 'one of the most delicate forms of adultery', contrasting it with the common, systematic, and sequential reading style. Just as Manuel learned to read in a way different from his usual style, we can teach readers to appreciate and embrace other forms of reading as well, one where breaks are welcome.

Figure 11 Social and material dynamics of early reading: collaborative reading fosters imagination, shared attention, and physical engagement with text.

Voice as an Empirical Phenomenon

While the debate on the materiality of text is emerging in reading research, the focus remains predominantly on the text itself, with materiality often reduced to the medium, that is, the text and its affordances for immersion or other forms of cognitive processes. While this perspective is important, it is too narrow. The process of reading extends beyond the physical text and its engagement with the hands; it involves a complex interaction between higher cognitive functions, embodied experience, and the broader text-environment. In contrast to a potter's engagement with clay – where the material visibly reveals the cognitive processes through its transformation – reading requires attention beyond manual interaction. Specifically, we must consider how the body itself functions as an empirical-material phenomenon, encompassing limbs, movement, and voice. Terence Cave, in *Live Artefacts* (2022), argues that language itself is material, and what we often perceive as immaterial is, in fact, observable in embodied forms of engagement:

> If language is not a material thing, one might ask, then what is it? As I write or think this sentence, shape it lovingly, delete it, rewrite it as if I were a potter shaping a ceramic bowl, is the act immaterial? If so, where is the immaterial domain? The alternative, which would perhaps be obvious if the Saussurean view were not the entrenched doxa that it still apparently is, would be to say that, if things shape the mind, they also shape language, and the shaping of language is 'like' the shaping of 'material' objects. I use scare quotes for 'like' because I don't think this can be reduced to a metaphor; both activities come under the rule of enactive cognition. And I use scare quotes for 'material' just to remind ourselves that, if there is no domain of transcendence, that word is a pleonasm. (Cave, 2022:49)

Extending this perspective, we can reconceptualise reading as an embodied process that includes not only manual and tactile engagement but also auditory phenomena and the physiological dynamics of the body, such as the movement of muscles, the mouth, and the vocal tract. Beyond physical objects, the stabilising and structuring effects of voice and gesture should also be recognised as integral components of material engagement. This is particularly relevant in the context of reading, where vocalisation serves as a creative means of producing varied expressions and emotions. Interestingly, in the following case where an adult woman reads Goethe's *Faust* in German, I observed that she shifted between silent reading and reading aloud. When asked why she did this, she replied:

> the fact that I hear it – the case that it is not just a voice inside my head, but I actually also hear it, allows me to focus my attention; that my thoughts so to speak are moved in the background ... I like to use multiple senses in some

> way to, well then that is the only thing I need to focus on, and I am not going to remember what I will be doing tomorrow . . . which I often do when I read inside my head. . . . I think German is awesome, I enjoy speaking it, so therefore it also . . . it is just cool I think to read it out loud and hear it, and at the same **time feel it in the mouth**, how the words kind of feel. (see, Trasmundi & Kukkonen, 2024:115)[10]

In this example, the voice, too, is perceived and engaged with as an empirical phenomenon, which becomes attractors of experience. Crucially, prosody is unmarked in alphabetic writing, but the readers I engaged with, reveal how they use it in rich – or creative – ways. In other research, Kristiansen et al. (2024) described how readers rely on extra-textual resources to go beyond the information given by linking imagined experience with felt reactions – rather than using conventions for instance – because there is no alphabet-based evidence for how prosody is articulated. The authors illustrate this point with an empirical study of voiced reading, where readers meet unusual place names:

> When readers encounter new words, they *can* apply abstract rules, but it seems instead that they enact their default language or produce non-standard tonemes when needing to read them out loud in a literary text. Names often reflect particularly local linguistic and cultural customs, and while these names might be glossed over in silent reading, reading out loud brings the reader into a confrontation with at least its linguistic form. (Kristiansen et al., 2024:8).

Altogether, reading is more than just decoding – it is at its core an imaginative process shaped by prior knowledge, affective engagement, and creative exploration. While this section has primarily examined how imaginative engagement unfolds through embodied reading practices, it is equally important to recognise that imagination and knowledge are not separate domains but dynamically intertwined. For instance, when readers encounter unfamiliar words, novel ideas, or unexpected stylistic choices, their prior knowledge and embodied reading habits shape their responses. This means that the imaginative engagement facilitated by breaks, prosody, and interactive reading strategies is not merely an act of free creativity but a way to integrate new knowledge with existing cognitive and experiential structures. The interplay between imagination and memory allows literary experiences to be not only felt in the moment but integrated in ways that contribute to understanding. Rather than positioning imagination as separate from the acquisition of knowledge, we should view it as a fundamental mechanism through which new information is understood, contextualised, and made meaningful. When readers engage imaginatively,

---

[10] For an extensive analysis of this reader's aesthetic reading experience see Trasmundi & Kukkonen (2024).

they do not abandon knowledge-building; rather, they actively structure and reconstruct their understanding in ways that allow them to retain not just factual information but complex reflections, patterns, and insights that shape their cognitive landscape over time.

One of the key insights from studying break-based reading patterns is that many readers, particularly young children, already engage in highly imaginative, nonlinear reading behaviours before they are trained out of them. Playfulness and vividly paced reading rhythms are common in early reading experiences, yet educational practices often discourage these tendencies in favour of continuous textual reading. While fluency is necessary, there is a risk in treating imaginative exploration as a distraction rather than as an integral part of reading. The small, observable windows into break-based reading patterns suggest that readers can engage in these imaginative and embodied processes in functional ways. However, readers often do so implicitly, and on a developmental scale, come to perceive them as increasingly invaluable – leading to a decline in their distribution, frequency, and quality. This Element argues that bringing awareness to these moments – through education, guided self-regulation, and reader training – can allow individuals to cultivate a dynamic relationship with texts and thus avoid unconsciously suppressing imaginative engagement over time.

My aim has been to empirically and theoretically underscore how breaks enable processes of imagining – an aspect that has been largely overlooked – rather than to assess the actual content or quality of what is imagined. However, preliminary observations suggest that these breaks correlate with more vivid and engaging reading experiences, making them an essential phenomenon for both theoretical inquiry and educational practice (Toro & Trasmundi, 2024). Recognising and addressing the role of these breaks – not only when they are functional but also when they might disrupt the reading experience – is crucial for research and pedagogy alike. Moving forward, an important next step is to examine what exactly happens during these moments of imaginative engagement – how they function (or, at times, hinder) the reading process and the task at hand. In the final Section 4, I extend this discussion by considering the broader implications of my argument for education and research.

4 Reading the Future

4.1 An Educational Program for Imaginative Reading

In the first half of the twentieth century, the philosopher and educational reformer John Dewey argued for a theory of experiential learning. Central to Dewey's theory is the principle of continuity, often referred to as an experiential continuum (Dewey, 1997). This principle suggests that all experiences build upon previous ones and influence future experiences, meaning that learning is not a series of isolated events but a connected, ongoing process. However, as noted in the introduction, not all education fosters growth – learning can also take the form of miseducation, where misguided or harmful knowledge impedes development. This model of education resonates strongly with the ecological-embodied approach to imaginative reading that has been central to this Element's argument. While all reading involves some degree of imaginative engagement, not all reading grasps the imagination's full potential. Dewey's ideas remind us that the quality and depth of our experiences, including reading experiences, vary greatly, and that attention must be paid to the conditions under which this imaginative engagement can be best enriched.

This section synthesises the theoretical foundations laid out in Sections 1 through 3, presenting an educational program that operationalises the core insights into imaginative reading. The key focus is on cultivating new habits of reading, where breaks – moments of reflection and re-engagement with the text – become a pivotal element. These breaks, or ma, disrupt the continuous flow of reading and introduce opportunities for cognitive and emotional engagement. One critical concern is that pedagogical practices from the very beginning of reading instruction often (unconsciously) suppress moments for creative engagement. If early imaginative and exploratory experiences are consistently discouraged, children may come to view reading only as an exercise in information processing, rather than as an activity in which they can modulate their own engagement, adjust their pace, and dynamically shift between immersion and critical reflection. The current emphasis on fluency and continuous symbol recognition – while essential – can therefore inadvertently train children to shut down the very moments that correlate with joy, curiosity, and self-efficacy in reading as described in the previous section. It is important to clarify that a break-probing strategy in reading does not compete with fluency-building but rather complement it at different stages of reading development. Automaticity in word recognition, for instance, is essential for reducing cognitive load, allowing readers to engage with texts at functional levels (Stanovich, 1986), yet we have also observed how both becoming and expert readers benefit from the ability to regulate their attention and strategically integrate breaks in reading. This indicates that controlled breaks, such as pauses and changes in rhythmical embodied pacemaking are crucial for imaginative reading, rather than obstacles to it. In this sense, breaks should not be seen as disruptions to fluency, but rather as complementary mechanisms that serve to engage the reader in creative ways. Teaching students to balance fluency with reflective breaks may, in fact, enhance comprehension, as controlled variations in reading speed have been shown to influence retention and meaning-making processes (Kuhn & Stahl, 2003).

While this Element has focused on how breaks facilitate imaginative engagement in general, it is important to clarify that the role and function of breaks vary depending on the reader's level of fluency. The precise nature of these variations remains an open question for further research. However, the examples in Section 3 illustrate that readers across all levels – from emerging to expert – engage in imaginative processes that extend beyond mere symbolic understanding. This suggests that breaks play a significant role in fostering engagement across different reading proficiencies, shaping how readers interact with and understand texts.

Importantly, this Element does not suggest that self-elicited breaks should be encouraged at all stages of all reading or that they are always functional. Rather, it highlights their overlooked role and calls for further research into how different forms of regulating the pace – whether spontaneous or structured – affect comprehension, fluency, and engagement across developmental stages. Future pedagogical approaches should consider how young readers can develop an awareness of their own attention – learning to regulate and sense their reading flow, recognising when to explore a break, when to ignore it, and when to modulate their pace. This self-awareness of engagement rhythms – the imagination pulse – is an acquired skill of attentional sensitivity, and its development should be supported by empirical research that explores what young readers can manage and how pedagogical strategies can foster both fluency and rich imaginative interaction with reading material.

Crucially, I do not suggest that reading is a completely freeform activity where interpretation is limitless. Imagination, while generative, is structured by textual constraints, cultural contexts, and prior knowledge. Even in highly creative reading experiences, meaning-making is guided by the affordances emerging from the engagement with the text itself – such as its syntax, structure, and embedded references. Thus, imaginative reading does not imply a detachment from textual information but rather an enriched and dynamic engagement with it. Additionally, it is important to recognise that imagination and reflection in reading do not occur in opposition to structured comprehension and analysis. Instead, they function as integrated processes that allow the reader to navigate between different cognitive modes – moving between the literal and the imaginative, the material and the immaterial, the expected and the novel. This perspective helps clarify that breaks are not about maximising imaginative freedom at the expense of comprehension, but about fostering a more layered, engaged, and personally meaningful interaction with the text.

However, to turn this theory into a practical educational framework, two key areas must be addressed. First, educators and policymakers must recognise the importance of breaks in reading, understanding that these moments are not interruptions but essential spaces for imagination to grow. Second, there must be a greater focus on integrating the ecological-embodied model into everyday educational practices, with attention to how multiscalar attention, pacemaking, and material engagement can be taught and cultivated.

4.2 Multiscalar Attention

At the core of imaginative reading lies the capacity for multiscalar attention – the ability to integrate multiple scales. A reader might begin with a simple focus of symbolic words but, through careful attention, shift between different temporal and experiential layers: connecting the text to their past experiences, imagining future possibilities, and making sense of the social and cultural implications embedded in the narrative. The break, or ma, is an exceptional moment where these scales can be integrated and explored further – the reader, free from the momentum of the linear text and its style, can engage in reflective thought or aesthetic exploration, for example, by paying attention to sound, shapes, scents, memories, and so on. For example, consider a student reading a passage about a character facing a moral dilemma. Without modulation of reading flow, the student might simply follow the plot. However, by changing the pace – whether by slowing down, gazing up, or momentarily disengaging from the text – they become more attuned to both macro-level reflections (such as how the dilemma connects to broader ethical questions or personal experiences) and micro-level affective responses – a fleeting sense of justice or guilt, a sudden chill that heightens emotional arousal, or an unexpected feeling of attachment to a character. These in-the-moment breaks create space for embodied and emotional engagement, whereas post-reading reflection typically shifts towards more structured, analytical comprehension. Such structured activity is typically modelled through analytical questions such as, 'How do you think the protagonist feels?' or 'What is the right thing to do?' While these prompts encourage readers to connect the textual world with their own perspectives, they constitute analysis rather than reading itself. By prioritising intellectual interpretation, such questions risk over-intellectualising the reading experience, leaving little room for more subtle, embodied engagements – such as the sensory taste of words, the rhythm of language, or the flickering, affective nuances that arise in the moment of reading. Moments that we observed as truly emotional and joyful.

To integrate these brief yet meaningful moments, educators could design reading exercises that encourage students to capture their emerging connections during the act of reading. Instead of postponing reflection until after the reading, students could be encouraged to write down thoughts and judgements *as* they emerge, for instance using reading journals, capturing moments of engagement, reflection, and emotional response. This practice enhances not only comprehension but also transforms the reading process into a participatory dialogue with the text, enriching both the imaginative and cognitive dimensions of the experience. Further, these activities help students become aware of how they can shift between different levels of attention and understanding during reading, fostering richer and more imaginative engagement that resonates equally with emergent embodied emotions and logical analysis of information. It thus gives the readers a direct understanding that their reading is a creative process that transcends mere inferencing or linguistic meaning-making of written words. It links what they perceive with experiential and future timescales that create phenomena like hope, aspirations, uncertainties, and so on. They *do* the reading. This multiscalar integration enables the reader to generate novelties, new meanings, and connections, engaging in a dialogue with the text that is not limited to the words on the page or reduced to later analysis.

4.3 Pacemaking: Managing Rhythms and Tensions

Pacemaking refers to the way readers manage the rhythms of engagement and reflection during reading. As discussed in earlier sections, the concept of ma, derived from Japanese aesthetics and dramaturgy, emphasises the significance of living pauses, intervals and creation. These breaks are not empty voids; they are spaces where the reader can slow down, reflect, and recalibrate their relationship with the text.

In educational settings, helping students understand the importance of pacing in reading can significantly enhance their ability to engage with complex texts. Pacemaking is an attribute of human agency, but it can be treated as a skill that allows readers to consciously modulate their temporal engagement with a text, recognising when to slow down and reflect or when to let the narrative flow forward. Teaching students to play with embodied pace patterns in their reading can help them become more resilient and adaptable readers, capable of handling a wide range of textual demands – from the lyrical and poetic to the dense and theoretical. Students can learn to pacemake deliberately, and as the ability to move beyond the drive for efficiency – reading quickly and smoothly – and instead recognising that pauses are integral to cognitive and imaginative growth. These rhythms of reading allow students to experience texts more dynamically, moving between quick skimming and slower immersion. The idea is not to disrupt the flow for its own sake, but to create spaces where the reader's thoughts can gestate and evolve.

For instance, a teacher might guide students through an exercise where they pause after particularly striking or complex passages – whether a sound, word, sentence, or plot point – allowing time for reflection and creative association. Crucially, this does not need to be 'meaningful' in the traditional sense but fosters a heightened sensitivity to reading beyond a simplistic view. The goal is to help students develop an intuitive sense of when to slow down and when to move forward, encouraging them to navigate the text according to its imaginative and cognitive demands. This tension between movement and pause is a productive one: it allows students to explore ideas more thoroughly, notice nuances in the text, and generate their own understanding by integrating experience with a given task. It fosters resilience in reading, as students become more adaptable in their approach, able to engage meaningfully with texts of varying complexity.

These activities can be structured around guided prompts, encouraging students to dwell on certain aspects of the text, explore their emotional responses, or make connections with other texts they have read. Importantly, pacemaking plays a crucial role in cultivating the ability to tolerate ambiguity and uncertainty. Intentional pauses create moments of tension or unresolved ideas that require further reflection, rather than immediate resolution. A pause compels the reader to remain in a challenging or uncertain space – one that might otherwise be avoided by simply moving forward. By learning to engage with these moments rather than bypass them, students develop a nuanced reading practice that embraces complexity and interpretive openness.

4.4 Material Engagement: The Physicality of Reading

The theory of Material Engagement (MET) emphasises that cognition is not confined to the brain but extends into our interactions with the world. In the context of reading, this means that the act of bodily interacting with a text – whether it is turning pages, making annotations, or highlighting – plays a significant role in shaping cognitive and imaginative processes. Educationally, MET implies that we must reconnect readers with the materiality of reading. Encouraging students to underline key passages or take notes in the margins can enhance their engagement with the material. These practices activate different sensory modalities, making the reading experience more immersive and bodily vibrant. For example, Delgado et al. (2018) suggest that students who interact with texts – through annotation or note-taking – are more likely to retain information and develop greater insights. In digital environments, educators can encourage the use of tools like highlighting, commenting, and sharing annotations in collaborative spaces, thus creating a multi-dimensional reading practice where students can engage both individually and communally.

Furthermore, this material engagement is closely linked to the concept of breaks, or ma. Breaks in reading not only provide cognitive space for reflection but are often accompanied by shifts in material interaction, such as pausing to underline a key passage or turning back to a previous section. These motor actions reinforce the reflective space of the break, allowing readers to engage with the text in both cognitive and embodied, multimodal ways. We understand this intuitively, yet educators often rely on heuristics, offering generic instructions like 'take notes' without guiding students on what to focus on. Readers need to be taught not only what to pay attention to but also how pacemaking itself makes them aware of different rhythms in the text.

4.5 Practical Applications and Future Directions

To apply the principles of multiscalar attention, pacemaking, and material engagement in educational settings, we must move away from traditional, linear approaches to reading instruction and embrace a more embodied and experimental pedagogy. This pedagogy should be designed to include and cultivate imagination, reflection, and critical thinking. Importantly, imagining here is not measured in terms of impactful outcome, but instead in terms of the sensibility and awareness of attention to aspects beyond the text. Reading is not just a skill to be optimised but a process that shapes how we engage with meaning, and our environment. While fluency, efficiency, and comprehension have long been prioritised in reading research, this Element highlights an equally crucial but often overlooked dimension: the role of pacing, pausing, and embodied engagement in fostering a critical and curious connection to texts. This work suggests that certain reading practices – especially those that suppress exploratory engagement, imaginative attunement, and self-regulated pauses – can limit the depth of a reader's experience and learning. Future research should explore how pedagogical approaches can incorporate a balance between fluency-building and imaginative engagement, ensuring that reading remains not only a skill but also a meaningful, enriching process of relating. One promising direction for integrating imaginative reading with empirical models of reading is to align this framework with Art Jacobs' Neurocognitive Poetics Model (Jacobs, 2015). This model emphasises reading speed as a crucial parameter and highlights how cognitive-emotional interactions shape literary engagement. The intersection between the ecological-embodied approach and Jacobs' model offers a way to understand how breaks function not merely as moments of distraction but as integral components of an affectively and cognitively regulated reading experience. By incorporating such insights from neurocognitive poetics, future research could explore how pacing strategies influence the depth of engagement, linking subjective reading experiences with measurable parameters of reading fluency and emotional response. These insights could also be extended into educational settings, helping students develop both automaticity in reading and the ability to regulate imaginative engagement dynamically. Further research might also consider how this aligns with integrative frameworks that examine reading as a multimodal, embodied practice (cf. Jacobs, 2015).

By integrating the ecological-embodied model of reading into educational practices, we create a space for students to engage in imaginative experimentation with texts. This approach involves not just reading for fluency or comprehension but engaging with the experience of reading – acknowledging that reading is an embodied, multi-sensory, and temporally layered practice.

Ultimately, this shift in focus – from mere fluency to imaginative engagement – will cultivate a new generation of readers who are not only adept at understanding complex texts but also capable of rethinking and reshaping their own sensitivity *during* reading.

4.6 Conclusion: Cultivating Imaginative and Critical Readers

As we confront the complex challenges of the Anthropocene – marked by environmental crises, socio-political instability, and technological transformations – the need for imaginative and critical thinkers becomes increasingly urgent. This Element has proposed that reading, far from being an interpretive and mental activity, is one powerful tool for cultivating these qualities.

By focusing on multiscalar attention, pacemaking, and material engagement, educators can foster an imaginative approach to reading – one that encourages students not only to comprehend linguistic meaning, but to question, reflect, and imagine new vistas. Reading, in this sense, becomes a site of both personal transformation and social possibility.

In conclusion, the future of education lies in our ability to nurture readers who are not only proficient but also imaginative and engaged – individuals who can approach the world's complexities with creativity, empathy, and critical insight. The imaginative power of reading, as this Element has sought to demonstrate, holds the potential to shape not just how we read but how we live.

References

Anderson, M. L. (2014). *After Phrenology: Neural Reuse and the Interactive Brain*. Cambridge, MA: MIT Press.

Andrade, J. (2010). What does doodling do? *Applied Cognitive Psychology*, 24: 100–106.

Asma, S. T. (2017). *The Evolution of Imagination*. Chicago: The University of Chicago Press.

Baggs, E. (2021). All affordances are social: Foundations of a Gibsonian social ontology. *Ecological Psychology*, 33(3–4): 257–278.

Ball, L. J., & Ormerod, T. C. (2000). Putting ethnography to work: The case for a cognitive ethnography of design. *International Journal of Human Computer Studies*, 53: 147–168.

Barash, D. (1974). Displacement activities in a dental office. *Psychological Reports*, 34: 947–949.

Baron, N. S. (2021). *How We Read Now: Strategic Choices for Print, Screen, and Audio*. Oxford: Oxford University Press.

Baron, N. S., & Mangen, A. (2021). The decline of long long-form reading in higher education. *Poetics Today*, 42(2): 253–279.

Bateson, G. (1973). *Steps to an Ecology of Mind*. St. Albans: Granada.

Benne, C. (2021). Tolle lege. Embodied reading and the 'scene of reading'. *Language Sciences*, 84: 101357.

Bruineberg, J., & van den Herik, J. C. (2021). Embodying mental affordances. *Inquiry*, 1–21. https://doi.org/10.1080/0020174X.2021.1987316.

Buckner, R. L. (2010). The role of the hippocampus in prediction and imagination. *Annual Review of Psychology*, 61: 27–48.

Buckner, R. L., Andrews-Hanna, J. R., & Schacter, D. L. (2008). The brain's default network: Anatomy, function, and relevance to disease. *Annals of the New York Academy of Sciences*, 1124: 1–38.

Buckner, R. L., & Carroll, D. C. (2006). Self-projection and the brain. *Trends in Cognitive Sciences*, 11(2): 49–57.

Cave, T. (2022). *Live Artefacts: Literature in a Cognitive Environment*. Oxford: Oxford University Press.

Christoff, K., Gordon, A. M., Smallwood, J., Smith, R., & Schooler, J. W. (2009). Experience sampling during fMRI reveals default network and executive system contributions to mind wandering. *Proceedings of the National Academy of Sciences of the United States of America*, 106: 8719–8724.

Christoff, K., Irving, Z. C., Fox, K. C., Spreng, R. N., & Andrews-Hanna, J. R. (2016). Mind-wandering as spontaneous thought: A dynamic framework. *Nature Reviews Neuroscience*, 17: 718–731.

Cobley, P., & Siebers, J. (2021). Close reading and distance: Between invariance and a rhetoric of embodiment. *Language Sciences*, 84: 101359.

Collini, S. (2018). *Speaking of Universities*. New York: Verso.

Cowley, S. J. (2011). Taking a language stance. *Ecological Psychology*, 23: 1–25.

Cowley, S. J. (2021). Reading: Skilled linguistic action. *Language Sciences*, 84: 101364.

Darwin, C. (1871). *The Descent of Man, and Selection in Relation to Sex*. London: John Murray.

Dehaene, S. (2009). *Reading in the Brain: The Science and Evolution of a Human Invention*. New York: Penguin.

Delgado, P., Vargas, C., Ackerman, R., & Salmerón, L. (2018). Don't throw away your printed books: A meta-analysis on the effects of reading media on reading comprehension. *Educational Research Review*, 25: 23–38.

Dewey, J. (1910). *How We Think*. New York: Prometheus Book.

Dewey, J. (1997). *Experience and Education*. New York: Touchstone.

Dewey, J. (2010). *How We Think*. New York: D.C.Heath & Co Publishers.

Di Paolo, E., Cuffari, E. C., & De Jaegher, H. (2018). *Linguistic Bodies: The Continuity between Life and Language*. Cambridge, MA: MIT Press.

Farley, J., Risko, E. F., & Kingstone, A. (2013). Everyday attention and lecture retention: The effects of time, fidgeting, and mind wandering. *Frontiers of Psychology*, 4: 619.

Flaherty, A. W. (2005). Frontotemporal and dopaminergic control of idea generation and creative drive. *Journal of Comparative Neurology*, 493(1): 147–153.

Forgeard, M. J. C., & Kaufman, J. C. (2015). Who cares about imagination, creativity, and innovation, and why? A review. *Psychology of Aesthetics, Creativity, and the Arts*, 10(3): 250–269.

Frank, A., Gleiser, M., & Thompson, E. (2024). *The Blind Spot: Why Science Cannot Ignore Human Experience*. Cambridge, MA: MIT Press.

Gabriel, R. (2023). Epistemic cultural constraints on the uses of psychology. *New Ideas in Psychology*, 68: 100986.

Gallagher, S. (2018). Building a stronger concept of embodiment. In A. Newen, L. De Bruin, & S. Gallagher (eds.), *The Oxford Handbook of 4E Cognition* (pp. 368–382). Oxford: Oxford University Press.

Gerrig, R. J. (1993). *Experiencing Narrative Worlds: On the Psychological Activities of Reading*. New Haven: Yale University Press.

Gibbs, R. W., Jr. (2017). Embodied dynamics in literary experience. In M. Burke, & E. T. Troscianko (eds.), *Cognitive Literary Science: Dialogues between Literature and Cognition* (pp. 219–237). New York: Oxford University Press.

Gibson, E. J. (1965). Learning to read. *Bulletin of the Orton Society*, 15: 32–47.

Gibson, J. (1979). *The Ecological Approach to Visual Perception*. Boston: Houghton Mifflin.

Goodwin, C. (1994). Professional vision. *American Anthropologist*, 96(3): 606–633.

Graeber, D., & Wengrow, D. (2021). *The Dawn of Everything: A New History of Humanity*. London: Allen Lane.

Green, M. C., & Brock, T. C. (2000). The role of transportation in the persuasiveness of public narratives. *Journal of Personality and Social Psychology*, 79(5): 701–721.

Green, M. C., & Brock, T. C. (2002). In the mind's eye: Transportation-imagery model of narrative persuasion. In M. C. Green, J. J. Strange, & T. C. Brock (eds.), *Narrative Impact: Social and Cognitive Foundations* (pp. 315–341). New York: Lawrence Erlbaum Associates.

Hassabis, D., Kumaran, D., & Maguire, E. A. (2007). Using imagination to understand the neural basis of episodic memory. *Journal of Neuroscience*, 27: 14365–14374.

Hassabis, D., & Maguire, E. A. (2009). The construction system of the brain. *Philosophical Transactions of the Royal Society of London: Series B, Biological Sciences*, 364: 1263–1271.

Heft, H. (1996). The ecological approach to navigation: A Gibsonian perspective. In J. Portugali (ed.), *The Construction of Cognitive Maps*. GeoJournal Library, vol. 32 (pp. 105–132). Dordrecht: Springer.

Heft, H. (2020). Ecological psychology as social psychology? *Theory and Psychology*, 30(6): 813–826.

Hermans, H. J. M., & Hermans-Konopka, A. (2010). *Dialogical Self Theory: Positioning and Counter-Positioning in a Globalizing Society*. Cambridge: Cambridge University Press.

Hodges, B. H., & Baron, R. M. (1992). Values as constraints on affordances: Perceiving and acting properly. *Journal for the Theory of Social Behaviour*, 22(3): 263–294.

Høffding, S. (2018). *A Phenomenology of Musical Absorption*. Cham: Springer International.

Hutchins, E. (1995). *Cognition in the Wild*. Cambridge, MA: MIT Press.

Hutchins, E. (2013). The cultural ecosystem of human cognition. *Philosophical Psychology*, 27(1): 34–49. https://doi.org/10.1080/09515089.2013.830548.

Ingold, T. (2021). An Interview with Tim Ingold. www.youtube.com/watch?v=zaZy0NWQoKo. Accessed 30 September 2024.

Ingold, T. (2022). *Imagining for Real: Essays on Creation, Attention and Correspondence*. London: Routledge.

Ingold, T. (2024). On Being Tasked with the Problem of Inhabiting the page. *Social Epistemology Review and Reply Collective*, 13(2): 1–7.

Jacobs, A. M. (2015). Neurocognitive poetics: Methods and models for investigating the neuronal and cognitive-affective bases of literature reception. *Frontiers in Human Neuroscience*, 9. https://doi.org/10.3389/fnhum.2015.00186.

Jensen, T. W., & Pedersen, S. B. (2016). Affect and affordances: The role of action and emotion in social interaction. *Cognitive Semiotics*, 9(1): 79–103.

Jensen, M. (2023). 'Min kuglepen er en sporhund, når jeg læser': Et kognitivt etnografisk studie af læseprocesser. ['My pen is a tracking dog when I read': A cognitive ethnographic study of reading processes]. University of Southern Denmark.

Kieverstein, J., & Rietveld, E. (2020). Skill-based engagement with a rich landscape of affordances as an alternative to thinking through other minds. *Behavioral and Brain Sciences (BBS)*, 43:e106. doi:10.1017/S0140525X1900284X.

Kieverstein, J., & Rietveld, E. (2018). Reconceiving representation-hungry cognition: An ecological-enactive proposal. *Adaptive Behavior*, 26(5):147–163. doi: 10.1177/1059712318772778.

Kono, Tetsuya. 2022. A Meteorological or Oceanographic Approach to the Self: An Interpretation of the 'Gap' of Zeami. www.youtube.com/watch?v=RBFbaqFTYxg. Accessed 30 September 2024.

Kress, G. (2003). *Literacy in the New Media Age*. London: Routledge.

Kristensen, D.-T., Kukkonen, K., Eriksen, S., & Trasmundi. S. B. (2024). Voices in reading literature. *Language Sciences*, 106: 101664.

Kuhn, M. R., & Stahl, S. A. (2003). Fluency: A review of developmental and remedial practices. *Journal of Educational Psychology*, 95(1): 3–21.

Kukkonen, K. (2020). *Probability Designs: Literature and Predictive Processing*. Oxford: Oxford University Press.

Kyselo, M. (2018). The body social: An enactive approach to the self. *Frontiers in Psychology*, 5(986): 1–16.

Kyselo, M (2023). What self in self-organization? Engaging Varela's epistemology for the co-embodied self. *Journal of Consciousness Studies* 30(11): 80–103.

Lefebvre, H. (2004). *Rhythmanalysis: Space, Time and Everyday Life*. S. Elden, & G. Moore (trans.). New York: Continuum.

Levine, J. A., Schleusner, S. J., & Jensen, M. D. (2000). Energy expenditure of nonexercise activity. *American Journal of Clinical Nutrition*, 72: 1451–1454.

Linell, P. (2009). *Rethinking Language, Mind, and World Dialogically: Interactional and Contextual Theories of Human Sense-Making*. Charlotte: Information Age.

Macrine, S. L., & Fugate, J. M. (2022). *Movement Matters: How Embodied Cognition Informs Teaching and Learning*. Cambridge: MIT Press.

Malafouris, L. (2013). *How Things Shape the Mind: A Theory of Material Engagement*. Cambridge, MA: MIT Press.

Mangen, A. (2008). Hypertext fiction reading: Haptics and immersion. *Advances in Haptics*, 1(3): 86–104.

Mangen, A. (2016). What hands may tell us about reading and writing. *Educational Theory*, 66(4): 457–477.

Mangen, A., Olivier, G., & Velay, J.-L. (2019). Comparing Comprehension of a long text read in print book and on kindle: Where in the text and when in the story? *Frontiers in Psychology*, 10: 38.

Mangen, A., & Schilhab, T. (2012). An embodied view of reading: Theoretical considerations, empirical findings and educational implications. In S. Matre, & A. Skaftun (eds.), *Skriv! Les!* (pp. 285–300). Trondheim: Akademika forlag.

Manguel, A. (2014). *A History of Reading*. New York: Penguin Books.

Mason, M. F., Norton, M. I., Van Horn, J. D., et al. (2007). Wandering minds: The default network and stimulus-independent thought. *Science*, 315: 393–395.

McClelland, T. (2020). Self-representational theories of consciousness. In U. Kriegel (ed.), *The Oxford Handbook of the Philosophy of Consciousness* (pp. 1–44). Oxford: Oxford University Press.

Menary, R. (2007). Writing as thinking. *Language Sciences*, 29(5): 621–632.

Menary, R. (2010). Introduction to the special issue on 4E cognition. *Phenomenology and the Cognitive Sciences*, 9: 459–463.

Mohiyeddini, C., Bauer, S., & Semple, S. (2013). Displacement behaviour is associated with reduced stress levels among men but not women. *PLoS ONE*, 8: e56355. 10.1371/journal.pone.0056355.

Mohiyeddini, C., & Semple, S. (2013). Displacement behaviour regulates the experience of stress in men. *Stress*, 16: 163–171.

Morioka, M. (2015). How to create *MA* – the living pause– in the landscape of the mind: The wisdom of Noh theatre. *International Journal for Dialogical Science*, 9(1): 81–95.

Newen, A., De Bruin, L., & Gallagher, S. (2018). *The Oxford Handbook of 4E Cognition*. Oxford: Oxford University Press.

Noë, A. (2004) *Action in Perception*. Cambridge, MA: MIT Press.

Popova, Y., & Cuffari, E. C. (2018). Temporality of sense-making in narrative interactions. *Cognitive Semiotics*, 11(1): 20180007.

Ravn, S. (2017). Dancing practices: Seeing and sensing the moving body. *Body & Society*, 23(2): 57–82.

Rietveld, E. (2022). The affordances of art for making technologies. *Adaptive Behavior*, 30(6): 489–503.

Rosa, H. (2020). *The Uncontrollability of the World*. J. C. Wagner (trans.). Cambridge.

Schacter, D. L., Addis, D. R., & Buckner, R. L. (2007). Remembering the past to imagine the future: The prospective brain. *Nature Reviews Neuroscience*, 8(9): 657–661.

Stanovich, K. E. (1986). Matthew effects in reading: Some consequences of individual differences in the acquisition of literacy. *Reading Research Quarterly*, 21(4): 360–407.

Steffensen, S. V. (2013). Cognitive probatonics: Towards an ecological psychology of cognitive particulars. *New Ideas in Psychology*, 42: 29–38.

Steffensen, S. V., Döring, M., & Cowley, S. J. (2024). Ecolinguistics: Living and languaging. In S. V. Steffensen, M. Döring, & S. Cowley (eds.), *Language as an Ecological Phenomenon: Languaging and Bioecologies in Human-Environment Relationships* (1–26). London: Bloomsbury Academic.

Stewart, J. (2019). *Breathing Life into Biology*. Cambridge: Cambridge Scholars.

Thompson-Schill, S. L., Ramscar, M., & Chrysikou, E. G. (2009). Cognition without control: When a little frontal lobe goes a long way. *Current Directions in Psychological Science*, 18(5): 259–263.

Toro, J., & Trasmundi, S. B. (2024). The aesthetic dimension of reading: An embodied-ecological approach. *Ecological Psychology*, 36(1): 3–16.

Trasmundi, S. (2020). *Errors in Interaction: A Cognitive Ethnography of Emergency Medicine*. Amsterdam: John Benjamins.

Trasmundi, S. B. (2024). Becoming a reader: Dwelling within the page. *Social Epistemology Review and Reply Collective*, 13(3): 20–32.

Trasmundi, S. B. (2025). Reading as open-ended engagement. In B. Bausch (ed.), *Reading Reading* (pp. 1–8). Hamburg: Textam Verlag.

Trasmundi, S. B., Baggs, E., Toro, J., & Steffensen, S. V. (2024). Expertise in non-well-defined task domains: The case of reading. *Social Epistemology*, 38(1): 13–27.

Trasmundi, S. B., & Cowley, S. J. (2020). How readers beget imagining. *Frontiers in Psychology*, 11: 531682.

Trasmundi, S. B., Kokkola, L., Schilhab, T., & Mangen, A. (2021). A distributed perspective on reading: Implications for education. *Language Sciences*, 84: 101367.

Trasmundi, S. B., & Kukkonen, K. (2024). Aisthessis, aesthetics and cognition: Embodiments in reading. *Journal of Comparative Literature and Aesthetics*, 47(3): 103–119.

Trasmundi, S. B., & Steffensen, S. V. (2016). Meaning emergence in the ecology of dialogical systems. *Psychology of Language and Communication*, 20(29): 154–181.

Trasmundi, S. B., & Toro, J. (2023). Mind wandering in reading: An embodied approach. *Frontiers in Human Neuroscience*, 17: 1061437.

Trasmundi, S. B., Toro, J., & Mangen, A. (2022). Human pacemakers and experiential reading. *Frontiers in Communication*, 7: 897043.

Van Dijk, L., & Rietveld, E. (2020). Situated imagination. *Phenomenology and the Cognitive Sciences*. 24:455–477. https://doi.org/10.1007/s11097-020-09701-2.

Walsh, D. M. (2015). *Organisms, Agency and Evolution*. Cambridge: Cambridge University Press.

Wig, S., Trasmundi, S. B., Hakemulder, F., Holm-Torjusen, F., & Mangen, A. (2025). Flow and longform reading. Notes from an exploratory case study. *Cognitive Semiotics*, 18(1): 53–71.

Wolf, M. (2018). *Reader, Come Home: The Reading Brain in a Digital World*. New York: Harper Collins.

Wolters, A., Kim, Y. G., & Szura, J. W. (2022). Is reading prosody related to reading comprehension? A meta-analysis. *Scientific Studies of Reading*, 26(1): 1–20.

Zabelina, D. L., & Robinson, M. D. (2010). Creativity as flexible cognitive control. *Psychology of Aesthetics, Creativity, and the Arts*, 4(3): 136–143.

Zermiani, F. M., Dhar, P., Sood, E., et al. (2024). InteRead: An eye tracking dataset of interrupted reading. In *Proceedings of the 2024 Joint International Conference on Computational Linguistics, Language Resources and Evaluation* (LREC-COLING 2024) (pp. 9154–9169). Torino, Italia. ELRA and ICCL.

Acknowledgements

There is nothing quite like the smell of real paper, the weight of a book in your hands, or the tactile joy of scribbling thoughts by hand, even if half of them end up lost in the margins or mysteriously undecipherable. My love for the analogue world remains strong – yet, somehow, my computer – who has never known the satisfaction of turning a page – got to type it all out.

Reading is a paradox. It follows rules, yet every reader and every reading are different. It is structured, yet personal. It is bound by language yet set free by imagination. I have been thinking about this paradox for a long time. But where, then, should we turn to understand it? To linguistics, with its syntax and semantics? To psychology, which maps cognition? To literature, to philosophy? Each offers insights, but none have shown me how reading truly works. So, I turned to the act itself, making the paradox an empirical question: What do readers do? I found that reading is not mere information processing but an unfolding – a movement that opens new vistas. And crucially, it is not just about flow but about rupture, about breaks and shifts in engagement. Imagination does not simply fill the gaps; it thrives in them. Many of my colleagues share these interests, and I am grateful to Tim Ingold for our long discussions on the history, practice, and future of reading. His work has shaped my thinking, as have the conversations with Simon Høffding, Mats Haraldsen, Ed Baggs, Juan Toro, and Alva Noë. I also owe thanks to the three anonymous reviewers, whose sharp critiques and thoughtful guidance saved me from my worst excesses – sometimes gently, sometimes firmly, but always wisely.

Also, a special thank you to my academic friends, Anne Mangen, Paul Cobley, Harry Heft, Karin Kukkonen, Per Linell, and Sune Vork Steffensen for their generous, critical perspectives, and invaluable recommendations, which have left their imprint on this manuscript in ways both subtle and profound. I am also grateful to the *Centre for Human Interactivity* and, in particular, to the *Centre for Literature, Cognition and Emotions* (LCE) for supporting my travel to Japan, where I conducted ethnographic reading data used in this Element. I am further grateful to the Danish Research Council, whose funding of the research project *The Imagining the Power of Reading* (grant number: 1130-00008A) made it possible for me to travel and engage with readers across cultures and countries.

Most importantly, this manuscript would not exist without the many people who welcomed me into their reading lives. To the becoming and expert readers who invited me into their homes, and to parents and teachers who allowed me a glimpse into their reading practices – your openness and insights made this project meaningful and empirically rich. Your stories have shaped the very core of this work and developed my own experience as a reader.

I hope this Element will inspire readers across disciplines, cultures, and roles to rethink their own reading practices as well. More than that, I hope it will encourage new methods that embrace breaks in reading – moments that, rather than interrupting understanding, might actually expand it. If nothing else, may it serve as a small reminder that reading is not just an act of decoding words on a page, but a form of engagement that binds and bridges people, ways of attending, and ways of acting in the world.

To Martin–
whose heart once raced too fast,
shaking my rhythm,
only to remind me–
he is the pulse that steadies my own.

Cambridge Elements

Creativity and Imagination

Anna Abraham
University of Georgia, USA

Anna Abraham, Ph.D. is the E. Paul Torrance Professor at the University of Georgia, USA. Her educational and professional training has been within the disciplines of psychology and neuroscience, and she has worked across a diverse range of academic departments and institutions the world over, all of which have informed her cross-cultural and multidisciplinary focus. She has penned numerous publications including the 2018 book, *The Neuroscience of Creativity* (Cambridge University Press), and 2020 edited volume, *The Cambridge Handbook of the Imagination*. Her latest book is *The Creative Brain: Myths and Truths* (2024, MIT Press).

About the Series

Cambridge Elements in Creativity and Imagination publishes original perspectives and insightful reviews of empirical research, methods, theories, or applications in the vast fields of creativity and the imagination. The series is particularly focused on showcasing novel, necessary and neglected perspectives.

Cambridge Elements

Creativity and Imagination

Elements in the Series

Slow Wonder: Letters on Imagination and Education
Peter O'Connor and Claudia Rozas Gómez

Prophets at a Tangent: How Art Shapes Social Imagination
Geoff Mulgan

Visions and Decisions: Imagination and Technique in Music Composition
Bruce Adolphe

Item-Response Theory for Creativity Measurement
Nils Myszkowski

Design Thinking and Other Approaches: How Different Disciplines See, Think and Act
Nathan Crilly

Connective Creativity: What Art Can Teach Us About Collaboration
Austin Choi-Fitzpatrick and Gordon Hoople

Landscapes of the Imagination
Gerald C. Cupchik

Outsight: Restoring the Role of Objects in Creative Problem Solving
Frédéric Vallée-Tourangeau

Narrative Creativity: An Introduction to How and Why
Angus Fletcher and Mike Benveniste

Mechanisms of Change and Creativity in Nature and Culture
Arne Dietrich

Psychodrama: A Creative Method to Survive and Thrive
Hod Orkibi

The Imagination Pulse: From Flickers to Firestorms in Reading
Sarah Bro Trasmundi

A full series listing is available at: www.cambridge.org/ECAI

Printed by Integrated Books International,
United States of America